Other Books by John C. Mohawk

Basic Call to Consciousness (ed.)
Exiled in the Land of the Free (ed. with Oren Lyons)
*Utopian Legacies: A History of Conquest and Oppression
in the Western World*

First published in 2005 by
Mohawk Publications
224 Heath Street
Buffalo, NY 14214
Phone: 716 833 3481

Library of Congress Control Number: 2004117471
ISBN 0-9761279-0-3

Set in 12 pt. New Times Roman
Cover Graphic: Lisa Marie Spivak

In Memory of Many Teachers:

Albert Jacobs, Worthington Green, Ernest Mohawk, Ed Curry, Harrison Ground, Corbett Sundown, Roy Buck, Leon Shenandoah, Alice Papineau, Irv Powless, Sr., Demus Elm, Moses David.

IROQUOIS CREATION STORY

John Arthur Gibson and
J.N.B. Hewitt's
Myth of the Earth Grasper

John C. Mohawk

Mohawk Publications

Forward

Iroquois Creation Story follows an ancient myth of creation which was transcribed and published by a modern ethnologist at the end of the nineteenth century. J.N.B. Hewitt traveled to the Grand River country and collaborated with Chief John Arthur Gibson, a ceremonial leader of the Onondaga, to make a written record of the Iroquois cosmology. Chief Gibson was one of the spokespersons for the Council of Chiefs of the traditional government of the Six Nations Indian "Reserve" and was reported to be the last surviving individual trained to recite the tradition. The two worked together, one dictating, the other typing and making notes in the Onondaga language. When they were finished, Hewitt did not rush to publication although his colleagues continuously urged him to do so. The resulting report was not published until 1928 in the *Annual Report of the Bureau of American Ethnology*. It was entitled *Myth of the Earth Grasper,* named after a moment in the narrative when the Creator of Life scoops up a handful of earth and, showing it to his twin brother declares, "this is alive!" Chief Gibson passed away before it appeared. The work has been reprinted in very limited editions since then, and is available, when available at all, in rare book specialty stores and in research libraries.

Earthgrasper was written in a style which is no longer popular, and uses language which many students and young people are unlikely to be able to penetrate, even when they are aware of the importance of the material. It needed an editor, one who might consciously remove the various remnants of Victorian conventions and attitudes which sometimes surface in the original text along with some elements which clearly were added following contact with Europeans or people of European descent. This volume is an attempt to accomplish that work, but it is offered with the humble recognition that while removing one set of conventions, one necessarily replaces it with another. The *Myth of the Earthgrasper* is remarkable and would be of significant interest simply as a source of ancient Iroquois thought because of who Chief John Arthur Gibson was, and as an example of the work of John Napoleon Brinton Hewitt, the ethnologist who gathered the work.

The job of editor, which could never be accomplished perfectly, was to preserve the elements of the narrative in language consistent with that used at the end of the twentieth century. It was my goal to eliminate repetitive language, preserve as much as possible the elements of the narrative such that the original authors might recognize it as their own, to avoid as much as possible changing the spirit or intent of the story, and to add very few of my own thoughts. Above all, I tried to preserve the thoughts of the ancients. Because the tradition lends itself to a contemporary interpretation, I anticipate some skepticism about possible alterations to lend it a modernist, or even postmodernist, interpretation. I have tried to be transparent about my own interventions, albeit in subtle ways.

It has become popular in recent years, even in scholarly circles, to try to uncover materials from non-Western cultures which reflect the viewpoint of those distinct peoples more than they illuminate the skills and/or opinions of the anthropologists or ethnologists. This is not to diminish or trivialize the contribution of the professional, but rather to give it context and it is, as they say, a good thing. Early anthropologists went into the field to gather this material because they believed that the indigenous cultures were rapidly disappearing. They did not, for the most part, expect to find timeless wisdom in indigenous oral traditions. It was widely believed in professional circles that the record of human cultural evolution which these cultures were presumed to represent were in danger of being forever lost and collecting them was considered a way of preserving the human cultural heritage. Thus the act of preservation was, often, thought of as valuable, and the item collected was the fruit of that effort.

We can and should be grateful that such men and women labored under sometimes difficult conditions to preserve these kinds of materials while remembering that they were products of a distinct time and place which is separate from, and sometimes incongruous to, our own. A century ago, when ethnologists evaluated the content of these materials, they were often looking for ways in which the indigenous thought could be seen as similar to Western ideas and, when opportunities arose to suggest that such ideas had been found, the discovery was thought to reflect well on the Indians. At least some of the people who did so had good intentions because, in an age when a popular ideology exalting a supposed Aryan supremacy flourished, statements urging the existence of non-Aryan intelligence were progressive. Times have changed. There are contemporary anthropologists who value such works precisely because they are distinct from, and often have elaborate lessons unknown in, Western cultural values.

The ancient Iroquois had no way of recording their great stories on paper, even though there is some evidence they possessed a form of writing which utilized bark as a medium. It is little short of miraculous, given the dramatic pressures and disasters visited upon them during the first two centuries following European contact, that a storyteller of the stature and expertise of John Arthur Gibson would have been available to an ethnologist as late as 1899, and that someone with Hewitt's skills could have earned the confidence of that rare individual. Chief Gibson was nearly one hundred years old, blind, and gifted with the knowledge of nearly all of the oral traditions of his people. His trust in Hewitt was not misplaced because the manuscript is for the most part a record of his work as he intended. In the context of the times and the circumstances, Hewitt did a credible job trying to preserve the material transmitted to him. There were other people who knew versions and who recorded the myth and, because of the way such traditions were transmitted, there was no officially sanctioned version which in any way negated or diminished the importance of the others.

The search for a single authoritarian version is not only futile because such a version does not exist and, in the context of dozens or even hundreds of indigenous communities such as existed at the time of contact certainly never existed, it is also a search within the tradition of tendencies within Western culture to seek essential and immutable truths in the form of texts.

Hewitt and Gibson were certainly aware of the existence of other versions preserved in distinct languages among Seneca, Cayuga and other nations, and each offers contributions to Haudenosaunee thought and culture. Some of these other versions have surfaced over the years, and each makes valuable contributions to our understanding of Haudenosaunee thought and culture. The Gibson version is the longest and most detailed but not more or less than that. Elements of the story continue to surface.

The story of how *Earthgrasper* was collected begins somewhat in the tradition of great dramatic narratives when Hewitt, working by the light of oil lamps on an early typewriter, is found spending his days typing the words and phrases, line by line, from the words of this Onondaga chief, in a cabin in the very rural Grand River Country in southern Ontario several generations before the American public or even Hewitt's contemporary colleagues were ready to interrogate such narratives as sources not only of tribal wisdom but perhaps as sources of universal human enlightenment.

Despite all the information which came to light about the existence of an Iroquois cosmology, anthropologists, with the exception of Frank Speck, generally failed to see a connection between the cosmology and the ceremonial life of the Iroquois. This is interesting because one of the major themes of the narrative pointedly answers a central question about Haudenosaunee identity. Who are we? We are the people who carry on the tradition of ceremonials of thanksgiving. Why do we do these ceremonials? Because we recognize our great good fortune as receivers of the gifts of the Giver of Life. The people who composed this narrative did so to transmit that message to future generations. As long as there are Haudenosaunee people, the narrative tells us, they will perform the Great Gamble for Life. For as long as the Haudenosaunee exist, according to this tradition, they will remember this story.

Although nothing of this sort is absolutely impossible, it is extremely difficult to imagine that a story of this kind could be authored today and even more remote that it could be linked to a complex spiritual tradition as that practiced by contemporary Iroquois. While successive generations of storytellers "tweaked" its elements to make it relevant to their contemporaries, the vast majority of its content comes from a deep and misty past rooted long before the arrival of Europeans. In those days, the primordeal forest was a perceived as a distinct "world" composed of great trees and abundant wildlife such that one might encounter a wolf or a bear at any time. To compose the story today in such a way that it would represent the culture would require an audience which was already receptive to the idea that the beings of the sky world -- the celestial bodies -- not only possess consciousness but, were there to be communication between the world of humans and their world, there are some things which we might expect to find in those communications.

It is as though all this happened at some immemorial time in the past, and that the memory of it happening recounted its origins in dreams of skyworld beings which parallel our own sacred dreams, which command our attention, and which must be acted out. What did the beings which participated in bringing order to our physical universe want to tell us? How should we think of their existence? How can we embrace and be happy in a world of nature when we are all too aware of ways nature sometimes threatens human life and may one day bring extinction to all of life? Indeed, how can we be happy with a system which mandates our individual eventual deaths, and the deaths of everyone dear to us? Long ago, in a forest far, far away, these questions were pondered.

The story begins with a premise. If it were possible for the forces of the universe to converse with humans, how would they do so and what would be their message? To converse with humans, we would need to encounter beings with the capacity for human-like communications, and the beings of the sky world encountered here are certainly anthropomorphic enough in that regard. Every culture which attempts to communicate with the powers of the universe seems to invent beings — often gods, but in

contemporary culture a variety of aliens does the job —
which are more or less in some important respects similar
to humans. If those beings — spiritual beings when
encountered by humans in sacred dreams or stories —
communicate with our species, that message must certainly
be mixed. In this version, a vision or dream projecting life
on earth motivates the spiritual players who will become
the eternal cosmic family: Mother Earth, Grandmother
Moon, elder Brother Sun. This vision of life in a real world
comes with an unhappy warning label: such life in such a
world is not permanent.

Eventually, in a natural world, all living things will die
and be transformed. This is because it must be. Human life
could not have come to exist were it not for the wonderful
process of renewal, and although the days of each of us is
numbered, we are advised to be grateful for each day
because we are extremely fortunate to have the chance to
enjoy it. This is a message that the glass is half full, and
urges humankind to focus on its fullness, and to feel
fortunate for what we have. Immortality was never an
option. Mindful that nature sometimes acts in ways that
seem pitilessly cruel, tearing loved ones from our grasp
even when they have performed every requirement of
acknowledgment of the sacred, the culture concludes that
humans are nevertheless fortunate to enjoy all that they
have. It is the kind of message that comes from elders,
embedded here in a tradition which venerated its oldest
individuals.

Perhaps the story was an invention of a people who
did not live in a forest. Whereas many origin stories
describe a physical world familiar to its audience, including
islands or mountains or rivers which compose a living
landscape, *Earthgrasper* has relatively few such features.
Except for the references to muskrats and mulberries,
sunflowers and chestnuts, (things which could have been

added at some point) this story could have been told almost anywhere. Parts of it could be very ancient. We don't know. The only clue is that the idea of the earth as supported on the back of a turtle appears in other cultures on other continents. This could be coincidence, but the number of such appearances is certainly intriguing.

It is important that we remember this story is "literature" in the sense that it has been written down, but that for centuries it was experienced through the senses of the ear and not the eye, and that the experience of hearing something in a large group, as the story was intended to be told, is quite different from reading it in isolation, as is now done. The Iroquois traditionalists recognized that in storytelling it can be awkward to go back over a missed section, and they develop intense listening skills. They often sit immobile, their eyes closed, every bit of their energy concentrated on the words of the speaker. In this frame of mind, powerful images are remembered, and the story can be passed on more effectively.

That ancient way of telling stories, of course, has long fallen out of popular usage in the West. *Earth Grasper* is one of those meta-narratives which seeks to interpret the mysteries of human existence. Eons ago people looked into the blackness of the nightime sky with its pinpoints of light, the comets and the moon and sun, and asked themselves, "What is the meaning of all this? Why are we here? How did we get to be here? What is our role in the great measure of things?" Only a cosmology, by definition, can address such issues. Such a story was not intended to be a secret among a few selected individuals. It was heard by all, the young and old, together, as a group experience. In the same way that everyone who participates in modern American culture has heard of the child who was born in a manger, everyone in ancient Iroquoia heard about the woman who fell from the sky.

It is to questions about the meaning of existence that grand mythologies, sometimes called meta-narratives, turn their attention. Mythologies construct visions of the past which address the question about how the world became the way it is and, equally important, how we, as cultural beings in a certain culture, came to be the way *we* are. Such stories also urge upon us the expectation that things have been known to happen in a certain way, and are likely to happen in that way again.

Long ago, in preliterate cultures, such traditions were passed from generation to generation in elaborate but carefully constructed forms which sometimes existed for centuries. In Europe, mythological traditions were preserved in songs. Interestingly, Homer, the Greek culture-bearer, was also blind. His *Iliad* had been passed down for centuries before it was committed to writing. Indeed, there is evidence that it inspired the invention of the ancient Greek alphabet as a means to preserve it for all time. Similar traditions of mythological stories handed down over untold generations have been found in other places and were recorded, for example, early during the twentieth century in Serbia.

Something similar to that preserved the Iroquois oral traditions. Iroquois oral traditions are delivered in a spoken cadence which is quite similar to a form of song. The practice is to preserve such traditions through memory, and to deliver them through a speaker who is assisted by learned others who are available to make corrections or insertions as needed at a performance. It is likely that this system was in place when Chief Gibson learned the tradition of Earthgrasper, and the system has survived to preserve other traditions. It is a way of keeping the tradition quite consistent so long as it is alive and being practiced by a group through oral transmission.

Earthgrasper is a classic myth. It purports to explain

how customs arise which identify the relationships between humankind and certain celestial bodies. Here we find why the Haudenosaunee refer to the thunder as grandfathers, the earth as mother, the moon as grandmother, the sun as Elder Brother. The people who live on the earth, it is proposed, have relationships to the spirits of the universe which are of a certain kind, and the tradition addresses questions about how and why human beings came to be on the earth and how the various spirits and forces which support life were in the beginning. In *Earth Grasper*, the proposed answers to these questions are many and complex, but they offer an Haudenosaunee vision of humankind's role in the universe, and they call upon the bearers of the culture to join that vision, to act it out, to join in with a dream, and to form a society which reflects it and which has, as its duties, carrying forth the ceremonies which represent the activities which are taking place in the Sky World.

The purpose of the explanation is to give human beings an identity relative to the forces of the universe, beginning with the individual and radiating out to the earth, plants, animals, trees, birds, winds, sun, moon, stars, and the spirits which created life on the earth. The Haudenosaunee religion calls upon the Haudenosaunee to reenact the ceremonies which represent the relationships to the Creation, and *Earthgrasper* articulates where the ceremonies came from, where the clans came from, where the nations came from, and why.

Although many changes have take place in the ensuing centuries since the first European invasion of Iroquoia, and although few of the Iroquois remain on their ancestral lands, it can be said that one of the most remarkable elements of Iroquois conservatism has been the retention and continual revitalization of the Iroquois ceremonial life. For more than one hundred fifty years both the U.S. and Canada have implemented policies designed to forcibly acculturate the people, including boarding schools, compulsory non-Iroquois education systems, forced replacement of traditional governments and every conceivable way of bringing the kinds of changes which would cause a people to abandon the belief systems which render them distinct peoples.

One result is that it would not be an exaggeration to state the Iroquois creation story has not been recounted in a public ceremony in any longhouse in all of Iroquoia for something over one hundred years. The story of the woman who fell from the sky and landed on Turtle's back, initiating the creation of Turtle Island, is not recounted or read in the Iroquois communities except by a few souls who have access to research libraries and who make a point of studying Iroquois culture. This could change and, in the course of a revitalization of the culture, would likely change.

Nevertheless, the ceremonies articulated in this story continue to be practiced, and in some places more vigorously today than was true thirty or forty years ago. In addition to this, in recent decades a revolution in art has been brought about by young Iroquois who over the past thirty years have taken up the tools and materials of contemporary artists around the world and have fashioned many images which arise from this story. It has helped to place Iroquois art in numerous venues. In some communities, there is a vigorous effort to sustain the languages and emersion schools for youngsters and adults as well as language education in the public schools is behind a rebirth of languages which seemed, less than a few decades ago, destined for extinction. A revitalization of Haudenosaunee cultural traditions seems far more likely than was thought in the recent past.

It would be an Iroquois way of doing things to tell a story and to refuse to tell the listener what he/she should have learned from the story. The Iroquois pattern would be to tell a story and to ask the listener to use his/her own mind to see what they think the story means. This would most likely be done in a group which would then discuss various elements of the story together, somewhat the same way some teachers do in university classes today. Iroquois teachers of the traditions, in my experience, are willing to accept that different people at different stages of life are able to grasp and learn from different elements of a story at different moments. Their point might be only that the story should be told and discussed among the generations. In ancient times, when this story was recited, small children were present, as were great grandparents and those in between. If they followed Iroquois form, there was a discussion period about the various elements following each segmented recitation. Surely Iroquois winter nights, when such stories were intended to be told, were long. There was plenty of time.

The story itself has elements which are very serious. At first glance a story which includes a woman falling from the sky might sound like one intended for children. This is anything but a story intended only for children. Children can listen and get something out of it, but it is primarily aimed at adults and is not light entertainment. The story begins by recounting an element of Iroquois practice and thought. According to this story, the beings of the universe, long before the earth was formed, possessed consciousness and could communicate among one another. Like the Iroquois, these beings (called here Sky World Dwellers) believed in the power of dreams. These were beings we can recognize, gods whose faces we have seen in the night time sky, some of whom already had names. We called them, among other things, stars and comets, moons and the sun and it is known among the people that while they might appear to us in human form in a dream, they do not exist in human form in the cosmos.

These beings set into motion processes of creation which would ultimately create life on earth. According to this way of seeing the world, this set the stage for a philosophical view of life on earth, a philosophy specific in many of its elements to the Indians of the eastern woodlands. The story goes on through some elaboration to posit that humankind occupies a time and place in the universe which offers enormous good fortune. The Sky World beings collaborate in order to create the conditions for life on earth. Their intention is that there be beings on earth, human beings, who will appreciate the Sky World beings. These human beings were intended to acknowledge the role of the Sky World, and especially the Twin who created life -- known originally as the Master of Life.

The result of this raised consciousness is found in Iroquois ceremonials. These are ceremonials of thanksgiving. These ceremonials acknowledge that in the time of the primeval universe there was a very remote chance that a place would be created which could support life and that, given a consciousness of this, expressions of gratitude are in order. Human beings who experience life should be grateful. This is acknowledged in a series of ceremonials which span the calendar year in the form of thanksgiving rituals. These rituals are organized around things which support life on earth -- the earth itself, seeds, thunders, sun, moon, corn and beans and squash, berries, and so forth. It is a way of directing the community and individual thought to the universe both near and far. As the story unfolds in the Sky World -- we would probably think of it as deep space -- a series of events leads us to recognizable current era earth. Whatever the underlying themes are, it is important to notice that the fundamental message on the story's own terms is that human beings should be grateful that they live in a world in which nature provides a life for them.

This is obviously very different from a tradition which sees nature as dangerous and something which can and should be subdued and conquered. The Haudenosaunee, and other natural world peoples, call upon the powers of the universe in their prayers for medicine or good fortune or whatever such powers might be able to bestow. Western culture designates a call to the powers of nature as a belief system based on magic. European mythology, on the other hand, insists on a promotion of miracles. A miracle is an act by the *super*natural which creates a result not possible in the physical world. While the Haudenosaunee are focused on a real world, people who believe in miracles — in the possibility of the impossible — are not. It is possible in the real world to call upon the forces of nature, whether in the form of herbs or of more technologically created drugs, to cure or keep alive a mortally ill or wounded person. In this conversation, the so-called miracle drugs are actually magical. But it is not possible in the real world to bring a dead person back to life. For that, you need a miracle. The Haudenosaunee believe in the powers of nature, but they, like many people who share the belief, would be put off by the term "magic," which has become somewhat of a pejorative   term they would not adopt.

Somewhere in the dictionary is a definition of happiness which holds that happiness is a feeling of great good fortune. Our story holds that we have much that we should be happy about, and evidence of this great good fortune is the manifestation of the gifts of nature. But even these gifts of nature are part of a grander scheme. These are ultimately the gifts of the beings of the Sky World, those who conceived of and created that which we experience as nature. We are now able to see evidence of this great good fortune which positions us in a special relationship to that

XV

which is called nature. We are now urged to do more than give gratitude. We, the human beings, are urged to join in the sacred act. At the time of the ceremonies, the longhouse becomes a reflection of the Sky World, the dances here those done there. Thus the ceremony not only celebrates the gifts of the creation, those who participate with their bodies in the music and dance spend those moments recreating the Sky World on earth.

One of the most important of these ceremonies is the Peach Stone Game, or Great Gamble. It is a kind of dice game, played here not for individual possessiveness, but as a recreation of the game played by the Earth Grasper against his grandmother in the Great Gamble for Life. The first game symbolized the great good fortune of the winners. The peachstones danced to determine which mind would prevail on earth, the mind of the grandmother and Earth Grasper's brother who sought to consume the newly born living things, or the mind of the Master of Life who intended the human beings and the other species to carry out the vision from the Sky World?

Some scholars who have approached indigenous mythologies in the past have tended to do so with their own agenda. They have often sought to find things which are universal in the human experience, seeking material to explain group psychology, or looking for universal cultural heroes. Some have tried to find common strings in all mythologies, while others have tended to dismiss these kinds of stories as lacking universal human value. It is rare to encounter even a hint that the authors of such spiritual traditions might possess pragmatic motivations. This is true even though contemporary American philosophers acknowledge that America's only contribution to world philosophy, American pragmatism, was strongly influenced by Native American cultures. The general discourse on such matters suggests that spiritualism and pragmatism are of such distinct and separate paths that the two cannot co-exist.

Such coexistence might actually be one of the accomplishments of some, perhaps many, indigenous traditions. While *Earthgrasper* asks its listener to consider that the world exists as though there was some kind of ancient drama among powerful creator spirits, the culture ultimately urges that people believe relatively obvious things in a context. The earth is where we come from, Mother Earth. We exist with the support of many things, and the thanksgiving address lists many of them, including water, trees, grasses, food plants, sun, moon, and so forth. Hardly any one would argue with these things. But then there are beliefs which are not so apparent, and no one is compelled to believe in these things, although everybody sees that others do. In the Eastern Woodlands, prior to the introduction of compulsive Christianity with its rules that you must believe in this and that and nothing more, there was little to argue about in an indigenous community because one was permitted to act on any belief which was not harmful to others. Tolerance of others' beliefs is not a ideological impulse in a community where people live closely together and count on one another. It is a practical way of reducing conflict.

Pragmatic spiritualism addresses a problem that humanists and scientists have not. Scientists are forced, by the factual nature of their work, to come to conclusions which people who practice wishful thinking cannot accept. The earth is but a tiny speck in the universe, and life, especially human life, is statistically unlikely. All the world's civilizations have come into existence during an inter-glacial period which cannot last forever. Someday, the ice will return to much of the earth. This is not a message which brings converts into the streets for celebrations. On the other hand, life has been pretty wonderful, and we are wise to make the best of it. A pragmatic spiritualist could see the positive in that reality and could invent ways to understand it and to act on it.

One of the purposes of a cultural narrative of this sort is to urge the listener or reader to perpetuate the culture, to carry on its sacred traditions or stories. Since Haudenosaunee spiritual and political leaders had no coercive powers of the state, no dungeons or inquisition chambers, they relied on persuasion. The story they told was intended to collect some obvious truths into a collective wisdom about the arrangement humankind has with the universe.

The most important may be that it positions humankind in a positive relationship to nature, and it urges people to embrace the idea that the creation's gifts of all the things that support life is something that people should feel fortunate about. It opens doors to ways of thinking about the nature of the universe, about life and death, which can be particularly healthy. The Iroquois took this complex set of messages and formed traditions of music, dress, and dance to represent it. To live in an Iroquois culture is to be exposed to its rich cultural elements which call on the mind to achieve consciousness while providing textures of feeling which are not easily described but which were intended by those who fashioned the experiences.

Our story assumes that a people who have these very strong relationships to the Sky World beings, who have conducted the ceremonies and who have thought about all of these spiritual issues, will be on their way to becoming a good people. Nevertheless, as we follow the story, we will discover that humans have frailties, one of which is that they suffer periodic memory loss and forget to uphold their sacred duties. Even in our story, which took place far in the ancient times, people need to be reminded of the proper path.

Earth Grasper offers to us ideas which will be echoed in subsequent Iroquois traditions, notably the Great Law of Peace and the Good Message of Handsome Lake. Things flow from sources which have roots deeper than individual talents or society's gifts. They flow from nature, and the sacred beings who designed nature. If one embraces the initial premise, that human beings were extremely lucky that of all of the places in the universe, they have a home just the right distance from a sun of just the right intensity, that there is enough water, grass, and enough of everything. From there, it's a small step to accept that whatever created all that is a force of unexcelled sacred dimensions and the will of that force is something people should try to cooperate with to perpetuate life. The way a group expresses its cooperation is through ceremonies which recreate the conditions present when people first came to consciousness of these things.

Humankind's relationship to nature projected in this precolonial, pre-patriarchial, pre-modern story carries a fundamental and unchanging truth, but one which subsequent generations would need to relearn over and over. Humans exist in a context of nature, and not vise versa. Everything we have ever had, everything we have, everything we will ever have -- our health, our good looks, our intelligence, everything -- is a product not of our own merit but of all that which created our world. That which created our world is not society, but the power of the universe. Nature, which is the context of our existence, is sacred. A significant manifestation of nature, the regenerative power of life, is also sacred, and we who walk about on the earth are not without obligations to perpetuate this system, the "work" of the Giver of Life, in the greater scheme of things. Society, and all that society has produced, is a creation of the powers of the universe, as was the human genius employed in its construction.

This way of thinking appears repeatedly in this and subsequent Iroquoian traditions. They are powerful ideas in Iroquoia, transmitted in stories which, like these ideas, should not be lost. My goal is to present this classic Iroquoian teaching into a form which can be read and considered today. The commentary I have attached to the text is intended to help the reader contextualize the material. If it is of any benefit to people interested in these kinds of issues, the effort will have been successful.

ONE
IN THE BEGINNING

> .....
> He, who thro' vast immensity can pierce,
> See worlds on worlds compose one universe,
> Observe how system into system runs,
> What other planets circle other suns,
>
> ...
> Look'd thro'? or can a part contain the whole?
> Is the great chain that draws all to agree, -
> And, drawn, supports - upheld by God or thee?
>
> As of thy mother Earth, why oaks are made
> Taller or stronger than the weeds they shade.
> ...
> And all that rises, rise in due degree;
> Then, in the sale of reas'ning life, 'tis plain
> There must be, somewhere, such a rank as Man.
> ...Alexander Pope

It happened in ancient times that an older man undertook to create conditions which would bring spiritual power to his sister's two young children, a boy and a girl. It was customary that spiritual powers came to those who had been concealed from society, and the old man took the children and kept them in a hiding place where no one would see them.

"No one will ever see you in your childhood," he told

In the Beginning

them, "and therefore you will possess goodness of mind and will not be stained or in any way be evil. Not until you have grown to manhood and womanhood will you mingle with the people."

In time, however, the uncle returned with a message. "I am suffering because of past injuries and ill fortunes directed at me and I must soon pass away. When I am gone, take my body and place it at the top of the highest tree. If some trouble should ever happen and you need to hear my voice again, it will be possible to do so."

The girl, grown to a young woman, began to cry. "How can I do that, uncle? I can't climb the highest tree."

"You can if you must," he replied.

The old man then went to his sister, Elder Woman, the mother of the two children. "I am leaving everything to you," he said. "You must treat the children well because they are children of destiny. You shall not hear my voice again until after their destiny is completed." Then the old man fell silent, an illness overcame him, and soon he was dead.

The three survivors followed directions. Elder Woman fashioned a bark coffin, and the young man took the body and coffin and carried it aloft to the top of the highest pine tree where he laid the body to rest. She then continued as the Elder Man had instructed and concealed her son and daughter as before.

Soon a man approached her lodge. "Where has your family gone?" he asked.

"They are absent," she replied.

"I have come to you as a matter of great urgency. Our leader, he who is Guardian of the Standing Tree, sent me with the message that you are summoned to him. Now, tell me when your family will return. It is possible that we are all to receive a revelation from Elder Man, and it is also possible

In the Beginning

that no one should repeat what Elder Man has said to Guardian of the Standing Tree. We know, you and I, that your family has begun to visit Elder Man."

"'I don't know what I should do. Elder Man lies at the top of the tree and my children are in hiding."

"It is possible that they are included in the thing that is desired by the Keeper of the Standing Tree." Then the stranger departed.

As soon as he was gone the Elder Woman heard her daughter crying. She cried for a long time. "Perhaps," Elder Woman began, "you would like to see Elder Man."

"I can't climb the tree."

"I can carry you there," her brother replied.

He carried her aloft to where the uncle's body was tied to the tree and they removed the bark. When she saw his face once again, a peace came over her mind. Then they returned to earth.

Soon the stranger returned to the lodge to speak to Elder Woman. "Your family are the only ones who have not come to the place where our leader is giving his feast. It is necessary that at least one of you come so that the chief will be pleased."

"Who is it that has attended?" Elder Woman asked.

"You should go and find out. Then you can talk with him."

"All right. Let's do that."

Elder Woman and the stranger then went to the lodge of the chief. When they arrived, the stranger said, "I have brought this woman here as you asked. She is the mother of the children you wish to attend your feast."

"Everyone, all who live here, have attended the feast," the chief began. "But none of your family have come. I think you are very powerful. I think you have the power to tell me

In the Beginning

what is on my mind."

"Who," Elder Woman asked, "has come to this place?"

"All have visited here," he answered. "The suns and the moons, the stars and the trees, the bushes and the grasses, the animals and the birds, those who run about on the earth. The springs of water and the rivers and the daylight and the clouds and the corn, beans, and squashes. The tobacco plant and the thunders and the water, and the meteor."

"This is why you have come. There is only one lacking. Of all those who have been here, only the wind has not come. I also desire that one will come who will reveal my will. I will probably thrust through the ground all the things of this world and I will do this because all of these things have failed to aid me in this world. When this happens, new things will come forth and this world will be renewed."

"It will not be long," Elder Woman replied, "before my two children will come forward and will try to reveal your vision. Of course, my children are still quite young."

"That is all right," Hoda"he', Guardian of the Standing Tree said. "I will wait. Look now at the Standing Tree. All its blossoms are in bloom, and until the blossoms fall off, my feast will continue. The only thing that keeps everything in good order is that those enjoying themselves must keep things interesting and entertaining for me."

Elder Woman returned to her lodge.

"Your uncle needs you up there," the brother said, pointing to the tree.

"Do you know what our uncle wants?" the sister asked.

"I do know. Go at once."

The young woman climbed to the top of the tree where the uncle lay. When she approached the bark coffin,

In the Beginning

she asked, "Do you need me?"

"Yes. You must go to the lodge of the man who is Guardian of the Tree. The blossoms of that tree provide the light of this world. Go there, and tell him you have arrived. He will ask where you have come from. You must tell him you have come from the place where stands the standing tree. He will ask what brings you here. You will reply that only the feast has caused you to come. He will ask your name. You will say that you are called Awe(n)ha'i', Mature Blossoms. He will say, 'I am thankful. The purpose of my feast has been fulfilled. You shall take away with you all the things which I shall cause to pass from this world into the next.' Now you must listen to me. He will say, 'First you must prepare food for me.' You will make mush from chestnuts."

"When you do this," the uncle continued, "the mush will spatter and stick to your body. Do not cry out, even though it is hot. When it is cooked, he will call to him his two servants, two dogs, and they will lick away the mush. Have great courage. If you are able to stand it, you will have passed this test."

"Next," the uncle continued, "he will say 'I have dreamed, and in my dream the people have uprooted the Standing Tree of Fruits and Flowers. And I was aware that my wife and I sat ourselves at the place where the earth was broken through where the roots of the tree had been.' Do not falter when this happens."

The young woman then descended the tree and returned to her brother's lodge.

"It is time for me to depart," she announced. "I am going to Hoda"he' and his feast."

"This is the right thing to do," her brother replied. "I believe it will come to pass that you will depart this world. Someday you will remember me, and when you do you will

In the Beginning

address me as Earthquake and someday you will think of me and when that happens everyone who is aware of this will remember what happened here."

The young woman then set out on her journey and before long she arrived at the lodge of Hoda"he' who continued to host a feast. The Great Standing Tree was laden with blossoms and a host of people were present. She then entered his lodge.

"I am here," she said.

"Where are you from?"

"I come from the place where the tree of my mother's brother stands."

"Why have you come?" Hoda"he' asked.

"To attend your feast."

"And your name?"

"I am Awe(n)ha'i'. Mature Blossoms."

"I am thankful that you have arrived. Your arrival is the purpose for which I have held this feast. Now many have paid a visit to this place and now you shall take them all away with you. I have thrust all the things of this place through the ground so that all can be transformed and become renewed. Those things on the earth which are here will become renewed. Look! My Standing Tree now bears a mass of dead flowers!"

Then he directed her to a place he had prepared.

"I have a mat for your comfort. For a very long time I have expected you to arrive."

Awe(n)ha'i' sat in the place he had prepared for her.

"Now, I want you to prepare food -- a mush made of chestnut. When the food is ready, you and I shall eat."

"Where are the things I will use to prepare this meal?" she asked.

"Go," he replied. "Over there is a doorway and inside

In the Beginning

is everything you will need."

Awe(n)ha'i' took a pot, filled it with water, and put it over the fire. While the water heated, she cut chestnuts and pounded them into meal. When the water boiled she stirred the meal into it. The meal began to spatter and hot mush stuck all over her body. Although she was burned, she did not stop.

When the mush was cooked she removed it from the fire.

"The food is ready!" she announced.

Hoda"he regarded her. "What happened? What are these things that appear on your body?" he asked.

"This happened when I prepared the food," she replied.

"It is possible that my servants can clean this off," he said. Then he called his servants, the two dogs, and she saw that they were frighteningly large. The two dogs proceeded to lick the mush from her body and their actions were rough and painful, but Awe(n)ha'i' did not flinch or cry out.

When the dogs were finished, he said, "I am thankful that this matter is concluded." Then they ate.

"I'm sure you saw a large body of people assembled on the field. As you know, they are about to play lacrosse and their game will greatly entertain me."

A lacrosse game then began. During the course of the game, different people approached and spoke to Awe(n)ha'i', but she did not reply. When the game was over, all dispersed, and a man announced that they should assemble again the next day.

The next day the people assembled and again they played lacrosse. During the game Hoda"he' turned to Awe(n)ha'i'. "You should go to the spring and fetch some water." She took up a bucket and made her way to the spring. On the way she passed many people. On her return, one of the

In the Beginning

lacrosse players approached her.

"May I have a drink?" he asked. She handed him her vessel and when he finished he handed the rest back to her. "Nia'weh," he said, "I am thankful." She replied, "Ni'o. So be it." Then she threw away the remaining water and went back and filled the vessel with fresh water.

When she reentered the lodge, Hoda"he was angry. "You have done that which I have forbidden you. I instructed that you are not to reply to anyone who speaks to you."

"I will not do it again," she said.

"I tell you this," Hoda"he replied. "Your mother has not yet come here and confirmed what has taken place since you arrived. You should go back to her and in her presence confirm your promise."

"I will do it," Awe(n)ha'i' answered. She then gathered her things and returned to her mother's lodge where she reported everything that had happened since she had left home. When she finished, Elder Woman answered, "I have delayed this matter too long. Here is a basket of huckleberry corn bread. He is distressed that we have not followed custom and that I have not acknowledged your marriage to him. I shall go to him. You will wait here until my return." Then she arranged a forehead burden strap to carry a basket of bread, and she departed.

When she arrived at Hoda"he's lodge, Elder Woman placed the basket of bread before him. "I am here. And now I bring that which confirms your marriage to my daughter and that my daughter lives with you and that I agree to it."

Hoda"he' took out the marriage bread and held it before him. "Now things are made right," he announced. "The public has been waiting a long time and, as is custom, all will share in the acknowledgment of this marriage by eating some of the bread. Now I must tell you that once you departed, your

In the Beginning

daughter wandered from place to place. When you return home, you must tell her that she must come straight here, that she should not stop, not even to stand still, until she arrives. I will prepare for your journey a quantity of dried meat in exchange and when you arrive at your lodge you should, as is custom, share with all your people. Then all will be satisfied."

Elder woman then departed with the basket of dried meat. When she arrived at her lodge she told her daughter of her conversation with Hoda"he. "I have settled the matter of your marriage. Go now to your husband's lodge."

Awe(n)ha'i' departed for her husband's village. She had not gone far when she saw a man who looked exactly like her husband. "Are you on the way home?" he asked. "I have come to meet you." But Awe(n)ha'i' did not stop and she did not answer. After she passed him she turned and her eyes met his. Immediately, he transformed himself. He was Fox. She journeyed a distance longer and then she saw the form of her husband approach. "I have come to meet you," he said. But she did not speak, and she did not stop. In a moment she turned to regard him, and as she did he transformed before her eyes. It was Wolf.

Now she hurried on her way and was approaching her husband's village. Soon she saw him approaching. "I was worried," he said, "I thought something may have happened." But she did not stop, and she did not speak. And in a moment she looked to see him transformed. It was Bear. She saw him run away and disappear.

When she entered the lodge she said, "I have returned."

"I am grateful," her husband said, "that you have survived the ordeal."

She lived there with him for some time. When they slept, it became their custom to sleep with their feet sole to

In the Beginning

sole and when they arose to a sitting posture the air they breathed met and co-mingled.

After a time her body gave evidence that she would become a mother. As the time of birth approached, Hoda"he' announced, "I've had a dream, and as is our custom I want the people to guess what my dream is so that the vision of my soul can become real."

Hoda"he announced another feast. At this time all the people came forward and each individually shouted what they thought was his vision. "Tobacco," said one, and he waved the person away, indicating that their selection was incorrect. "Juneberries," said another, and they too were waved away. All the people and all the animals made their proposals. All were waved away. A great misfortune, a negative force, had made seemingly impossible that the vision would be found and his mind put at peace.

Finally, Fire Dragon (Comet), whose body was white, stepped forward. "I wish to try to find the word you seek. You have a need that we should uproot Tooth, the Standing Tree."

Hoda"he' arose with a great presence. "I am thankful," he said, "the suggestions of my vision have been fulfilled. Now I can tell you the rest. I saw that those assembled had uprooted the Standing Tree and I saw that I and my wife sat together at the opening thus made through the ground, our feet dangling into the chasm, and that we shared food as we sat there. I saw all the things that shall come to pass."

The people gathered around the tree determined to do what the dream had commanded. A number of them exerted a great effort and tore the tree from the firmament. The place where it stood was left a great chasm which reached through the ground to expose a void on the other side.

"Now it has come to be," Hode"he' announced. "The

In the Beginning

conditions which can create Fate have come to pass. Now the flowers of the tree which have illuminated this world for all time have become withered and all that exists here can become new. All things shall come into a constant state of unending transformation and re-transformation. Now my wife and I shall eat together at the edge of the chasm."

Awe(n)ha'i' then set food at the edge of the chasm and seated herself there. "Now the conditions of your vision are fulfilled," she said.

"Now all kinds of things that must come to be are fulfilled," Hode"he' said. "Now you and I shall eat together, as is required." When they had eaten, he stood and turned to his wife. "Now you must depart from here," he said, and he thrust her into the chasm and she disappeared from sight. The man-beings then replanted the Tree of Light.

As her body was sinking through the darkness she saw Fire Dragon (Comet) and he seized her body in flight. "Are you traveling?" he said. "I will aid you as best as I can in all things so that you can survive when you arrive below. The reason am doing this is that your former husband accused me of those things for which he cast you from the Sky World. He accuses us of trying to frustrate the fulfillment of his vision. I am bringing with me what you will need to live in this new place."

She saw that he held dried corn and dried meat, and she took both.

"I will travel with you," Fire Dragon said, "but halfway I will turn back." And soon he was gone.

Soon she heard another voice, one of the dwellers of the Sky World who had been cast out previously. "It will not be long and all will become here as it was in the place you have left." And the voice became silent and all she heard was a sound in the blackness like the sound of the pumpkin rattle.

In the Beginning

There appeared below her an endless black sea and also below were many waterfowl of all kinds. One of them a Man-Duck, cried out, "a Being is falling from the sky!" And Loon replied, "Come, let us rise up to meet her and bring her gently down!" And they did. She seated herself on their united bodies. Loon gathered all the Water-Fowl Beings together as they carried the Sky World Woman about. "We are all assembled, we who were once of the Sky World and who arrived here first. We should help so that this woman can survive here."

And so the various Water Fowl Beings put their minds together, but they were not able to formulate a plan to help the woman. "Something must be done," said Loon, "to keep her body from sinking." Then Hanoghye (Muskrat) said, "I will dive to the bottom of the water to bring earth for her. It is well known to us that she has creative power and can use this earth."

Hanoghye disappeared beneath the water and was gone a long time. Finally, as the woman circled overhead on the bodies of the Water Fowl Beings, Hanoghye came to the surface. He was already long dead, and the others pressed forward for the cause of his death. Nagayagih (Beaver) came forward to try to help. He searched Hanoghye and found he held earth in both paws and in his mouth.

Now Hahowen said, "Now we need a volunteer to hold up this earth so that we can put this woman down." Beaver offered to try. They put the earth upon his back, but after a short time he cried out. "I don't think I'll be able to do it. It is too heavy."

Then Hanyadengona (Great Turtle) stepped forward. "I will try," he said. Then they placed the earth upon his back. After a short time he said, "It is all right. I will be able to hold it. And if it happens that the earth shall continue to grow in

In the Beginning

size, I too will grow in size with it."

Now Hahowen spoke:

"Perhaps we who came first have done all we can do and have fulfilled our destiny in regard to this woman." They placed the woman on the earth on Turtle's back, and then they went away.

The material upon which the woman rested -- earth -- continued to grow. As the earth reached a suitable size, Mature Blossoms gave birth to a baby girl, and she cared for the child, and the child grew rapidly. It was not long before the child was a young woman.

This young woman enjoyed exploring the Turtle Island. One day, she was startled to see a man watching her. The man said, "Would you not agree to marry me? It seems that you are seeking someone." The young woman examined him very carefully and she saw that his clothing was yellow in color.

"Of my own will I would never answer you. I must discuss this matter with my mother," she said. "If it is to be, it is she who must will it." She then turned about and went home. When she saw her mother she told what had happened.

Mature Blossoms said, "You did the right thing." When the young woman related that the clothing of the man was yellow, Elder woman said, "I will not consent to your marriage to him." Soon the young woman was back to the place where she had seen the man. "My mother will not consent," she said.

"I am not insulted," the man replied. Then he turned to depart. The young woman watched him as he moved away and in a moment she saw him transform. He was not a human being. He was Fox.

A few days later the young woman went out to fetch wood. As she was bundling the wood, a man appeared and

In the Beginning

said, "Would you marry me?" She regarded him and saw that his body was dirty and the flaps broad on his leggings, and his mantle had deep scallops all around. The young woman replied that her mother must decide, and she returned to Mature Blossoms and gave a report.

Mature Blossoms said, "I am thankful that you accomplished what you did. It is well known that individual is invulnerable. I consent that you shall marry. Invite him here."

The young woman returned to the place she had seen the man and confronted him again. "My mother assents to our marriage," she said. "She wishes to invite you to our lodge."

"I can't come with you right away," the man answered. "First I must go home and make preparations. When I have completed, I will come to the place where your lodge stands, but I must say that I will not come to live with you two. I will only visit there."

When the young woman returned to her mother, Mature Blossoms asked, "Where is the man?" The daughter replied, "He returned home. There he will visit the place from which he started, then he will come, but only for a visit. He will not settle down here."

"It is as I have said," Mature Blossoms remarked. "He is invulnerable. He is a Turtle Man." The two waited for the man to come. When it grew dark, the two prepared to sleep.

Just after they had gone to bed, the man entered and said, "I am here." The two listened closely. "I must tell you what must be. I will leave my arrows here through the night. Early tomorrow I will come for them." The young woman saw two arrows. One had a flint point, and one had no attached point. As she watched, he repeatedly straightened a third arrow which also had no attached point. Then he

In the Beginning

approached and laid two arrows on her body side by side. "Leave them this way during the night. Do not undo them until I come again and I will undo them." Then he left the lodge and went home.

Early the next day he removed the two arrows then returned home. At that time, it is said, the young woman was very happy. Soon she became aware that her life had changed, and Mature Blossoms said, "We are fortunate. You will have a child soon."

Soon it was evident from her appearance that she was about to be a mother. At that time, she was surprised to hear two male voices conversing from within her body.

The first voice said to the other, "What will you do after you leave this womb and we are born?"

The second answered, "I will create human beings and they will live together as groups. And I will create everything that human beings will need to live by and the things I create will make these human beings happy to live upon the earth. And what will you do?"

"I will make the attempt to do as you say. It must come to pass that I will have an impact on the earth."

When it was time for them to be born, one said to the other, "which of us shall go first?"

The young woman-being heard this conversation.

"You go first," the first voice said. "As for me, I see light here, and I shall exit through this spot."

As the other began to depart, he called back, "Do not do this. If you do, you will kill our mother." Then the first twin was born. In a moment, the second male child emerged from his mother's armpit. As Young Woman gave birth, she died.

Mature Blossoms then took the twin boys and she placed them under the bed. Then she attended her daughter's

In the Beginning

body, placing it at the entrance to the bark shelter and saying, "In ten days she will rise up again."

The two male children were healthy and large in size and they continued to grow very rapidly such that within a few days they were able to converse with Mature Blossoms. Then Mature Blossoms said, "Do you know where you have come from? And do you know where you will go when you leave this place?"

One said, "I know. We have come from the Sky World, and I will remember that. I will continue to grasp with both hands the knowledge of the place from which I came. And when the time will come, I will go back to that place."

Mature Blossoms was pleased. "You know the entire matter," she said. "I will name you De'hae'hiyawa"kho(n) -- he holds the sky -- Skyholder." Then she asked the second twin the same question.

"I'm not thinking about that, and I'm not thinking about where I am going in the future. I am thinking only about that which my father left me," he replied.

"And what is that," she asked.

"He left the arrow which has a point on it for me," he answered. "It is obviously intended for me to defend myself. That is why I am thinking of nothing else."

"Therefore," Mature Blossoms rejoined, "I shall call you O'ha'a', Flint."

In a few days, Mature Blossoms overheard the two boys talking.

"Do you know where our mother is?" Flint asked.

"I know only that she is sleeping,"Skyholder answered.

He turned to Mature Blossoms and asked, "Is it true she sleeps?"

"It is true," she answered.

In the Beginning

"It is important," Flint stated, "that I see our mother."

"You will see her," Mature Blossoms replied, "When she rises again."

"You must know," Flint said, "but it will ease my anxiety to see her myself."

Mature Blossoms could see no harm, so she took the boys to the doorway and showed them the body.

When Flint saw her, he said, "Why are you sleeping there? Get up." But she did not move.

"What can we do with this sleeping woman?" Flint asked.

"This is how things are," Elder Woman replied. "When it is time, she will rise again."

Skyholder said, "it doesn't bother me that she sleeps until it is time for her to arise."

"I will wait but a short time," said Flint. "If she doesn't arise when I want her, then it won't matter to me if she never arises again. For now, I am going to wander about so that I can entertain myself." He then left to wander from place to place.

Mature Blossoms loved her grandsons to different degrees. She loved Flint very much, but her love for Skyholder was reserved. As soon as Skyholder had left the lodge, Elder Woman said to Flint, "I have very little food and I don't know when or how I will be able to get more. You and I will share what I have. Every day our situation is becoming more serious."

"I will go and look for something for us to eat," Flint replied.

"Whenever your brother leaves, you and I will eat. Whatever is left over we will give to him," she said.

"Can you make a bow and arrow for me," he asked. "I will," Mature Blossoms replied. "And a fine bow and arrow.

In the Beginning

But whatever happens, do not lend it to your brother."

Soon Skyholder returned and saw that his brother had a bow and arrow. "Where did you get this?" he asked.

"My grandmother made it for me."

Then he turned to his grandmother and asked, "would you also make a bow and arrow for me?" Mature Blossoms replied, "it is enough that you two have a bow and arrow between you." Skyholder did not ask again.

In a few days, Flint had attached an arrowhead to the arrow. Then he went to the place where his mother lay and said, "I am going to awaken you, mother. You have been asleep for a long time and unless you wake up, I am going to shoot an arrow through you." Then he shook her for a long time and when she did not arise, he shot an arrow through her. When she did not stir he then destroyed her body.

When Skyholder returned, he was distressed. "You have destroyed our mother. She took the lead in establishing a home here on the earth, and she was the first to depart from this earth. She shall be called She Leads and she will be remembered for what she accomplished."

After a while, Skyholder approached Mature Blossoms and said, "it is not good that you treat my brother and I differently. I should have a bow and arrow also." And Elder Woman consented and made for him a bow and one arrow. "But if you lose it," she said, "I will not make another."

Skyholder continued his habit of exploring. One day, as he was going along the shore of a lake, he spotted a huge bird he had never seen before. Immediately he took his bow and arrow and stalked the bird until he saw that it came to rest in a tree. Then he took aim and shot at the bird, but missed. As the bird flew away, he watched his arrow fall into the water. Realizing that if he lost the arrow his grandmother would not make another, he waded into the water after it.

In the Beginning

Soon he disappeared into the lake and then, to his surprise, there was suddenly no more water in front of him. Instead, there was a lodge and a man sitting before it.

"For a long time I have watched you," the man said, "and I need to meet you. I caused you to come here. The reason I did this is because your grandmother does not respect you."

"Now it is time for you to begin the work which is your destiny. First I must tell you that it is a serious matter that you and your brother have developed differences of mind," the strange man said.

"There are many things which I must give you which will be for you to live on," he continued, "because your grandmother denies you the things necessary to your sustenance." He then motioned to a large store of food, offering Skyholder to take what he would. "Now you will eat, and you will have provisions. And when Flint and Elder Woman see that you have food, they will come and ask you for some. When they do, you will urge upon them that they must have patience and must take care how much they eat."

"I am here to tell you that you have the power to create for yourself those things you will need. All kinds of things will come to pass according to your desires. If it happens that you will need anything, you must come back here again." Skyholder acknowledged all he had been told.

"I must go home now," he said. Before he left he received a quantity of seed.

When he arrived at his grandmother's lodge he was once again offered the food which was leftover from the meal she and Flint had eaten.

"Grandmother," Skyholder asked, "why is it we never eat together? Why do you always give me dry things to eat?"

"It is because we are so poor. I generally find only old

In the Beginning

bits of food to eat."

"Grandmother, now I am about to set out on the work which I am to do."

"Perhaps this means you will build a lodge for yourself," she said.

"Yes, that would be appropriate." He then journeyed to the other side of the island and there he built for himself a bark lodge. Now he began his work.

He made the grass. Then he created and planted a sunflower near his lodge. "This," he said, "will be a sign to the human beings when they are established here on the earth."

He made red willow. "I have planted a medicine which shall be the oldest of all," he mused. And he created strawberries, which bear fruit close to the earth. And he made thimbleberry, and mulberry. "I shall plant that which shall be called huckleberry," he said, and it came to be.

In the Beginning

TWO
TWINS

Skyholder busied himself creating all kinds of plants which provide what we know as foods. Then he decided he should eat and rest before finishing his work. He built a fire and began roasting his latest creation, corn.

It was at this time that the wind began to carry from his fire a very appetizing aroma. Just at that time Flint was walking around outside and it happened that he could smell the aroma of roasting corn. In a moment he told his grandmother about the aroma and she directed him to follow it to his brother's lodge.

Soon he arrived at its source. There he found Skyholder roasting an ear of corn and as he watched it seemed that streams of oil were dripping from the cooking ears. "What are you cooking?" he asked.

"I am preparing food which will sustain human beings who will live on this earth in the future," was the reply.

"Can you spare me some?" Flint continued.

"It is not yet time. Soon food will be plentiful on the earth and then all who have need may eat."

As Flint turned to go he looked all around his brother's

Twins

lodge. To his astonishment he saw many things growing and many of these had produced flowers. He saw a beautifully colored shrub and asked, "What kind of thing is this?"

"I have planted that. Soon it will bear fruit."

Flint returned to the lodge of his grandmother and told her all that he had seen. "You must keep watch," she said, "and when he is gone from his lodge, alert me and I will come to see these things."

At that time Skyholder returned to the underwater lodge of the strange man -- his father. The man soon issued a warning. "Your grandmother is set against you and your work and she will try to undo what you are doing. I will tell you what you must do. When Flint next visits, he will ask for corn. Tell him you would trade the corn for the substance of his life -- the thing contained in his body. He will agree, and you will see that substance -- the flint -- come forth from his mouth. When you see the flint, seize it and pull it until you think it is as long as the arrowhead he carries and then say, 'break it here!'"

"He will say, 'break it yourself,' but you are not to do so. It must be he who breaks it off. When he does so, take it. Only that will make it possible that you will be successful in what you are doing and he will not be able to spoil your work. He will attempt to take control, but he will not be able to do it when you control the substance of his life."

Skyholder then returned to his lodge and again began to roast ears of corn. Flint once again sensed the odor and, without telling his grandmother, went to the lodge of his brother.

"What you are making smells good," he said. "Can I have some?"

"That which you want you may have if you should give to me the flint -- the power to freeze living things."

Twins

"Do you mean the point on my arrow?" he asked.

"I mean the thing contained in your body."

"O.K.." And he opened his mouth wide and out came forth a lethal weapon which looked like flint. Now Skyholder grasped it and pulled it forth and said, "Now here is where it should be broken off."

"Then break it off," Flint said.

"You own your life. You shall break it off yourself and give it to me. Then we have a deal." Flint then broke it off.

"Now you have what you want," Flint said.

"I accept it and now I will give you what you asked for," Skyholder replied. At that time he plucked off two grains of corn from the roasted corn at his fire pit. "You will eat one, and give one to our grandmother."

Flint then returned to his grandmother's lodge and there he told of all that had happened. He gave her the kernel of corn and each of them ate their single kernel of roasted corn.

The old woman ate and said, "This tastes good. This tastes very good! You will tell me the next time you sense your brother is making food and I will go there."

Meanwhile, Skyholder went about his work. The trees and shrubs he had planted had produced fruit. Now he created the bodies of the bluebird and the robin and pine martin and said, "I have finished your bodies. I have planted things so that you can reproduce here on the earth. It is a suitable place for you to have offspring."

He had made two of each, one male and one female. When he let them go, they flew and they also sang with beautiful voices. Soon Flint also heard and saw them and he reported this to his grandmother, who once again determined

Twins

to visit Skyholder's lodge.

Skyholder continued his work. He created the body of the deer and then the moose and the buffalo -- two each, one male and one female. "I have completed your bodies," he said, "and I have planted things here on the earth for your use." And he let them go and they ran away.

Then he created the bodies of two passenger pigeons -- a male and a female. And he created porcupines, and wild turkeys, and the bear and racoon families and when he was finished he turned and went to his lodge where he once again cooked for himself.

Flint sensed the aroma of cooking food and he also could sense the ripened shrubs of the plants his brother had created. He went to his grandmother's lodge and said, "Grandmother, I can smell all kinds of sweet aromas."

Elder Woman was curious. "Now we must go to Skyholder's lodge to see what kinds of things are going on there," she said. As they traveled, she was surprised at all the sweet aromas in the air caused by the many fruits of Skyholder's creations.

She saw the sunflower growing at Skyholder's door. Nearby they saw a plant bearing fruit which was covered with drops of syrup -- raspberries. The two visitors entered the lodge and there they saw him roasting something. Fatness flowed from the ears and into the fire in streamlets.

"Who made the thing which stands outside?" she asked.

"I made it," Skyholder said. "I just started."

"Would you share with us some of what you are cooking?" she asked.

"Certainly. But it will not be possible to share of one tree which stands outside." Then he gave each a grain of corn, and they ate.

Twins

"Let us go out," Skyholder said, and the three left the lodge. "This is the first thing I planted, it is called sunflower." Then they moved on.

Before they had gone far, he showed them another plant. "This I call red willow," he said. "And this is called thimbleberry." He plucked one off for each to eat.

"This growing here is called mulberry," he said, and again he picked one for each to eat. "Now let us go back." On the way back he stopped. "Now this is called huckleberry," he announced, and gave each one piece of the fruit to eat. "Thus it shall be on the earth that each shall ripen at a different time."

"It is extremely wonderful and pleasing to the mind what you have done here," Elder Woman said. "Would it be possible that we could take some of these back with us?"

"That will not be possible because I have just planted them," Skyholder said. "But in time they will be abundant, and then you can take what you want."

"And who was it that created all these birds and animals?" she asked.

"I did," Skyholder stated. "All is a product of my own labor."

"And why did you do these things?" she asked.

"Soon this earth will have people," Skyholder said.

"Now we will return home," she said, and the two departed. When they were at their lodge, Elder Woman said, "It is extremely wonderful, the things he has done. He said he would make the things that are necessary, and he has done so."

"Grandmother," said Flint, "I also have the power to do what my brother is doing."

Soon they heard a loud sound approaching and they

Twins

went to see what was happening. As they stood outside they were amazed to see a herd of deer pass by. Soon they saw other animals in great number passing their lodge. There were many bear, and many elk. Animals made great noises with their feet and their wings and their voices, and many languages were heard in the air.

"It is as he has planned," she exclaimed. "The beings that Skyholder has finished are now able to reproduce themselves and multiply."

"I will go to the place where he does this work," Flint proposed, "and I will find out where he gets the material he uses to finish the bodies of all the animals he has created. He has completed all kinds of fruits, too. If he will tell me how he does this, I too will make these things because he has been stingy and hasn't given us very much. I will make these things and you and I will live in the presence of abundance."

Soon Flint went to the lodge of his brother.

"I have come with a purpose," he began. "I am seeking to know what kind of thing you used to make all these many things you have now planted about this place, and the various kinds of game animals you have completed."

Then Skyholder took up a handful of earth and held it out to his brother and said, "I tell you that the earth is alive! Now you must understand that I took earth and from it I created all these things that live. I made all the things I have planted and I have finished the job of creating the living bodies of all the plants and that is why they live and it is also why they, individually, will die and become earth again. The same is true of the animals."

"This information is what I came for," Flint replied, and he then turned to go back to where he came from.

"I also have a question," Skyholder said. "What kind of thing would kill you?"

Twins

"Only two things," Flint answered. "All I fear is flint stone and the deer antler. Nothing else." Then he went home.

When he reached home Flint spoke to his grandmother. "Now I know what he uses to create all this life. He uses earth. Now I have a plan. I think it would be easy to conceal all the game animals so they would be under our control."

"How will you do that?" Elder Woman asked.

"I will open a mountain and capture them and hold them there."

Then he went to a cliff which was set against a great mountain and he set about the work of building for himself a great cavern. Then he gathered up all the game animals and herded them into the cavern and he placed a huge rock at the entrance so none could get away.

"Now," he said, "I have brought all under my control. Now I can get that which I and my grandmother need without any problem."

Then he went to the lodge where he and his grandmother lived and he told her what he had done.

"It is extremely fortunate," she said, "that we have the meat we need in abundance."

Then he went to the lodge of his brother. When he arrived, he found Skyholder busy making many arrows.

"Why are you making all these arrows?" he asked.

"Soon the game animals will be in great abundance."

"I have not seen them lately," Flint replied.

"As you know, they do not stay in one place. Perhaps they are now somewhere a distance from here."

Flint then went to the lodge of his grandmother and told her what happened. In time she told him they were out of

Twins

meat, and he went to the cave and opened it and killed an animal. Then he closed it and brought the meat back to the lodge. Thus he and the grandmother lived for a period of time.

Skyholder soon became aware that the animals were no longer present. He went to the place where his father dwelled under the water. "I do not know what has happened to the animals."

"I know what happened. Your brother has outwitted you. He has captured the animals and hidden them in a great cave. There the animals now abide. This cave is near the lodge he occupies and it is hidden by a great rock which covers the entrance. Go there and watch him. When he goes to the cave, follow him, and when he leaves, release the animals."

When the time was appropriate, Skyholder did as told. He first gathered up all his arrows and he went to the mountain and hid himself there. In time Flint came toward him and then he went past to the mountain and to the great rock which concealed the cave. When he arrived, he looked around to see that no one was watching, then he moved the rock and entered the cave. Skyholder watched from a distance.

In time he emerged from the cave and he carried with his burden strap the body of a huge porcupine and he spoke. "It was with great difficulty that I killed this game animal, and it almost killed me." Then he moved the rock and once again closed the cave.

As soon as he was gone, Flint emerged and moved the rock and released all the game animals. "I completed your bodies, but it has not been good that you have not become difficult to catch. So now I give you an instruction, that as long as the earth shall exist you shall do your utmost to be certain that no one should see you. You will be free, and it

Twins

will be because of your own efforts that you shall remain free." Then the animals all dispersed and disappeared into the forest.

Then Skyholder shot a deer with his arrow and the arrow became fixed in its body. "Go to the lodge of my grandmother." In a moment, at the grandmother's lodge a sound of hoofs was heard and the sound of a body crashing to the earth outside the doorway. The grandmother rushed to the door. "What is happening?"

She was surprised to see a deer at her door. "Look, Flint, an animal has visited our lodge."

Flint came to inspect the deer and he found the arrow and recognized it as one belonging to his brother. He said nothing.

Then Skyholder shot a racoon and a bear and ordered them to also go to the grandmother's lodge. "Now perhaps that will be sufficient," he said.

Twins

THREE
TWO ISLANDS

Flint immediately recognized the arrow in the animal's body as one belonging to his brother, but he said nothing and he and his grandmother retired to the lodge.

Skyholder was not finished. He shot a buffalo, and the animal ran and fell at the door of the lodge of the grandmother. He repeated this feat with a bear and a moose and a duck until, finally, he pronounced, "Now perhaps that is enough" When he arrived at his grandmother's lodge, she said, "A wonderful thing has happened. While you were gone your brother went out to hunt. Look at the animal he has killed and brought back."

"It is a porcupine," Skyholder observed. "Actually, where he has gone there is no game. But look, I have been out hunting, and animals are plentiful where I hunted."

Then he proceeded to clean and dress the animals and he cut up the bodies and hung the pieces about the lodge. Then he brought the skins into the lodge and he fastened these against the wall of the inside of the lodge and placed skins under the bed of the grandmother.

"Now my promises are fulfilled," he said. "You will be the first whose mind is made satisfied by the things which

Two Islands

live on this earth. One day human beings will be born here on the earth, and they too will find happiness from the things the earth shall continue to bring forth. Now, when the things I have brought you and my brother are used up, you will find that there is plenty to meet your needs and you will continue to have your minds at peace"

Skyholder decided to leave. Soon be was thinking about the behavior of his brother. "Perhaps, it would be better if he and I were separated. His actions distract me and make my work more difficult." He went to the edge of the waters in the floating island and he cut the island in two, thrusting water in between so that no one could cross from the one to the other. When he was finished with this work he said,"Now my brother and I are separated."

Sometime later Flint announced to the grand-mother, "We have only a small supply of meat remaining." Then he left the lodge to go hunting. He went from place to place, but he did not find any game. Finally, he grew very tired, but just then he saw some animals. When they saw him, they quickly ran away and he could only watch when they plunged into the water and swam away. As he watched, for the first time he saw the island on the other side where the animals went.

"I must tell Skyholder" he thought. "He probably doesn't know about this." But when he went to find the lodge of his brother, he could not find it. And he couldn't find his brother, either. He searched the whole island, then he went home. When he arrived, he told his grandmother all that had happened and that his brother had disappeared and an island had appeared and the animals were gone.

"I can do nothing about all this." she replied.

"I can. I can do what Skyholder has done. I can create animals. I will begin with small animals."

He took and shaped earth in the form of butterflies and

Two Islands

when he was finished they flew away. They were imperfect, and he would call them moths.

Then he looked about and he saw the birds his brother called the passenger pigeon and he took up earth and he fashioned these pigeons. He finished them before he became aware that these creatures had bodies covered with fur and possessed teeth and then they flew away.

Then Flint decided to create that which he saw growing next to his brother's lodge and which Skyholder had called sunflower. He fashioned the plant as best he could, and placed it near his lodge. Then he continued his work, creating the bodies of small beings and when he did this these small beings rose up into the air and flew away.

Soon he was startled to see his brother approaching from the distance. "What are you doing here?" Skyholder asked. "And what were those beings I saw flying from here as I approached?"

"These are the small animals I am fashioning," he said. Skyholder regarded these creatures."These are beings which will assist me," he said. "They will be called flies, and they will live on the bodies of game animals."

"Come and see," said Flint. "I have planted sunflower." The two went closer to the lodge, and there stood the plant Flint had finished.

"This is a plant that grows a flower, and several kinds of animals will be able to live from this plant," Skyholder announced. "It will be called thistle."

"Come, there is another that I have made that I wish to show you, though I may have made a mistake." Flint led the way to the flying creatures which had grown fur and teeth "It would not be good," said Skyholder, "if creatures such as these were together with the feathered creatures. Just as the earth is divided into a period of time during which there is

Two Islands

light and another during which darkness prevails, so shall it be with these creatures. The creatures with fur and teeth which fly shall be called bats, and they will inhabit the night time, and the creatures with feathers shall inhabit the daytime." Flint was astonished at these words.

"Now I must return to my lodge to continue my work." Then he went to his lodge. There he contemplated creating an orb which would be a source of light for the earth below, but for this job he needed advice. He then went to the lodge of the strange man who lived beneath the water.

"I have come to this place to discuss my plans to create an orb of light to be present so that there will be daylight for the earth."

Then the man answered, "It is time that I tell of these things. Your grandmother's brother awaits in that place where she originally came from. He is now ready, and he expects her to remember him. In the beginning he said, 'When I am remembered, the earth shall quake,' and when his younger sister departed he said, 'Someday I shall go to inspect this place where you have gone.' It would be a good thing to invite him here. Now here is what you must do.

"You have created the red willow. Take two pieces of that. From one, scrape the bark and make a tea you will use as an emetic. With the other, scrape the bark and put it in the fire. When the smoke rises, leap into it and say, 'Now, Elder Brother, you and I shall meet!' It will come to pass that he will meet you half way between earth and the skyworld. Then you will tell him what you need. He will listen to you, for he has great power."

Skyholder returned home and did exactly as he was told. After he had taken the emetic and as the smoke rose he leaped into the fire and said "Now I go there!" And he went upward. He had gone but a short way when he saw a man

Two Islands

approaching him, and the man said, "Now we have met. What is it you want?"

"I need help. I have completed many things on earth, but now the light provided by the sunflower is not sufficient, for the earth has grown very large. Now there are two floating islands, but I think I will add to these and there will be more. So now I will need to give daylight to the whole world. Earthholder sent me here."

"I have watched you for a long time," Elder Brother replied, "and long have waited for someone to remember me. I am fully prepared for this matter. I will attach my body to the underside of the skyworld. I will start at this place, and return to this place each day. I will care for these things you will leave on the earth. It will be this way for as long as the earth shall exist."

"Now that which I have needed is provided," Skyholder said. "From this time forward sunflower shall continue to measure your approach when you give daylight.

"Now we must think of other things" the man said. "Your brother cut off the head of your mother. That is all that is left of her at your grandmother's lodge. Your grandmother is my dear younger sister. If it pleases you, perhaps you could assign your mother a duty to move about and she and I would help one another. The things Flint is doing and will do should cause you anxiety. He plans to upset and make a mockery of your work. You did a good thing in separating yourself from him. It will cause him difficulty."

"He and I will settle the matter between us,"Skyholder replied. "Wait and do not attach your body as you have described until you hear from me. Then the people who will be present will know of your power."

"I am called Earthquake. Someday, at the end of the world, the earth shall shake. It is then that people will give me

Two Islands

a name."

"At midday," Skyholder announced, "you will be halfway on your path. There you will rest for a short while as you regain your strength. This will be a significant thing for the people who will live on the earth. Whatever is occupying their minds, their thinking shall be directed to you at midday, and when this is done it will continue always to be good, for you will have time to consider their thoughts."

"This is how it will be for as long as the earth continues. The families of human beings on the earth will continue to say, 'He, our Elder Brother,' when they talk of you. Now you and I must separate. Tomorrow you will come up over the horizon for the first time, and you will cause it to be daylight." Then Skyholder returned to his lodge.

When he arrived at his lodge he said "Now I will make human beings," and as soon as he had said this he made the body of the first human being. "This earth I have in my hand is really alive, and so is the whole earth, and the bodies I make from it will continue to live." Then he made the flesh of the human being. At that time he took a portion of his own life and put it in the body of the human being, and a portion of his own blood and enclosed it in the human being's flesh. Next he took a portion of his power to speak and enclosed it in the throat of the human being. Now he placed his breath in the human and the human being came to life and arose and stood before him.

"Now you may see all that I have created here," Skyholder announced. "I have placed you on the earth so you can beautify it by cultivating it." At that moment he saw the Elder Brother come over the horizon and daylight appeared and it was beautiful and agreeably warm.

"You can see that orb of light," Skyholder continued, "and it shall forever be for you an object of thought. It will

Two Islands

bring pleasure to your mind, and it will bring warmth to the days and next to them, to the nights. Also it will provide warmth and light necessary for the animals and the plants to live, and for you human beings to live, also."

"You will travel about on the earth as long as there is daylight. And when darkness comes, you will rest, and the animals will rest from time to time. In this I have completed something which will continue into the future for as long as the earth exists."

When the daylight spread across the earth, Flint and his grandmother became aware of it. Flint determined to go to his brother to find out more about what was happening. But as he traveled to his brother's lodge he found that the water which separated the two islands had grown wider and the other island was now barely visible. He looked about and found a birch tree and from this he took bark and made for himself a canoe and set out across the water.

When he arrived at the other island he stepped out of the canoe and immediately a saw a human being for the first time. "Where did you come from?" Flint asked.

"I came to life in this place," the human being answered. "Who created your body?"

"The one who finished my body lives near here." The two then journeyed to Skyholder's lodge. "Did you finish the body of the human being I just saw?" Flint asked.

"I did."

"Then it is you who caused all this daylight."

"It is Elder Brother who cause this," Skyholder replied. "Come, let us walk about that you may see what has come to be." As they walked along Flint saw that the fruits and flowers had increased greatly in number, and that there were a great variety of animals, and many in number were they."The earth continues to grow, and these growing things

Two Islands

increase in size and all will become numerous. In the beginning the human beings were few in number, but in the future they too will become numerous."

Flint then returned home where he reported all he had seen to his grandmother, including the story about the Elder Brother. "Now the thing is fulfilled," the grandmother said.

"Long ago, when I departed from home, my elder Brother said, 'I will one day come to wherever you are,' and now he has come. He who is known as Earthquake is my Elder Brother. So he is referring to his relationship to me when he says he is Elder Brother."

Now Flint said, "I will also make a human being. By the time my brother arrives, I will have completed this task." Then he went out. Flint set out about the work of fashioning a human being as he thought one should be.

As soon as he was finished, he spoke to the body he had made, saying "Now stand upright and walk." But the being instead leaped from his grasp and went into the water where he quickly disappeared. In a short while he thrust his head out and Flint said, "Come!" But he did not answer and he did not move.

After a time, Flint was convinced he had made a mistake. "I did not do a good job creating his body, so I must try again." So he made another, and when he was finished he said to his creation, "Stand upright, walk!" And the creature stood upright and went to a tree and in a moment had climbed to the top of the tree.

Flint reflected on this event and said, "I have once again made a mistake. This being is too small, and his tail is too long. Come down!" he said, but the creature would not stir. Then Flint said, "Now I shall make another, this time a much larger being."

Now he made another. As soon as it was completed,

Two Islands

he said, "Stand upright. Walk!" This time the being stood upright. "Now, go from place to place," Flint commanded. And when he saw that the body he had finished now walked, he asked, "Could it be that I have done something correctly? Now I will make another, a game animal."

And he made another. As soon as it was completed, he said "Walk. You shall be called deer." And now the being did arise and did run away and it cried out as it did so. Now he set about to make another and when he finished he said, "Arise." And when it walked away he said, "You will be called bear." And the being ran away.

Now Flint saw that Skyholder was approaching. When he arrived, Flint said, "Now I shall show you what I have done," and the two commenced walking about. Soon they arrived at the lake and Flint said, "There is the human being I made." When Skyholder spoke to the being, saying, "Come and walk," the creature cried out and leaped into the water out of sight. "That is not a human being," Skyholder continued "it will be called frog."

"I have made another human being," Flint said, and the two continued their walk. Soon Flint pointed upward, saying, "See, there he sits." Fur grew form his body, and a tail. "What kind of thing are you, sitting up there?" Skyholder asked, but the creature cried out and wept. "We will call you Monkey, because you weep so easily," and the two went on. A short distance away Flint said, "There sits a human being."

"What kind of thing are you who sits on the ground?" Skyholder asked, and the creature burst out in a loud sound and wept. "We will name you ape." Then Flint said, "There are two more I wish to show you," and so the two went on. Soon they saw two animals. "This one is called deer," Flint offered, "and this one is bear."

"This is not a deer," Skyholder rejoined. "This we will

Two Islands

call wolf. And this one we will call Grizzly Bear." The two of them then returned to their lodges. Flint then said to his grandmother, "I showed Skyholder the human being I made, and the deer and the bear, but he did not confirm them. He said I did not make them properly.

"I shall make bodies of more beings, and I will send these to the island where he inhabits, and these beings will eat all those things my brother has now completed. And if he is offended by this, then he and I will fight as a last resort. So tomorrow you and I will go to his lodge."

"I will not go with you to his lodge," grandmother stated, "unless you can show me how we are going to cross the water."

"I will solve this problem. I will cause a bridge to float, and we will walk across on that."

When nighttime came, Flint turned to the powers of the night, saying, "Black Night, you have the power that, were you a being like me, you would be able to create a bridge between these islands." And it began to grow very cold and the cold increased until the approach of daylight and a bridge of ice appeared.

When he saw these events Skyholder thought, "Perhaps Flint will have the power to spoil all those things I have planted for it is he who has caused all this cold. He has increased his power by means of darkness, so now I must assign someone to see that it does not become excessively dark or excessively cold."

Early in the morning the two approached Skyholder's island.

"How did you manage to cross the waters?" Skyholder asked.

"Your brother made a bridge that floats, and we crossed on that," grandmother answered.

Two Islands

Now Flint was becoming nervous and morning dawned and the earth began to grow hot.

"You and I have to go back soon," he said. "Soon it will not be possible for us to cross."

"It is up to Skyholder," the grandmother said, "to send us back. We are, after all, his guests."

"I will prepare food," Skyholder said. "We will eat the fruit which I have planted and which is now ripe. After we've eaten, we shall tour this place and I will show you all the new things."

Then he brought corn and roasted it and the aroma of corn was exceedingly pleasant and the juices flowed from the ears. "Would it be all right," the grandmother asked, "if I take a single grain and eat it?"

"It is not our custom," Skyholder said. "We must wait until it is cooked. We will eat it together. It is well known we all have an equal right to it."

The old woman asked, "It is such a small matter that you should let me have the small undeveloped end of the ear."

"It is not a custom which should come to pass," he replied.

Skyholder replied, "We will be together when we eat, and each will have an equal right to the food."

"I can't believe how stingy you are," the old woman said. Then she went to stand near the fire and she picked up a handful of ashes and she threw them on his roasting corn. As soon as she did this, the appealing aroma ceased and she said, "Is it only human beings who should be pleased. Is it not possible that I should ever be pleased?"

"What you have done is not good," Skyholder rebuked.

"You have spoiled something which will bring happiness to people."

Two Islands

When the corn was cooked, they ate together. When they finished, Skyholder said, "Now I will show you all the things that are growing here."

Two Islands

FOUR
THE GAMBLE FOR LIFE

"Even if the universe is the result of a cosmic throw of the dice and not deliberate creation, then we have won an incredibly important jackpot, a universe that has the potential for almost limitless creativity."
Mallary, *Our Improbable Universe*, 16.

They went out and a short distance from the lodge they found a tree which bore large fruit. The fruit was slightly sweet and Skyholder said, "This is called apple. We shall each pick one and eat together," and they did so.

"Would it be all right if I pick one to take with us?" Mature Blossoms asked.

"No one should pick it until it ripens. Then you can pick all you want. The animals will also eat some at that time."

Mature Blossoms then turned around and re-entered the lodge where she picked up a handful of ashes from the fire and she soon stood by the apple tree and threw the ashes on the unripe fruit. At once it grew black and sour. "You are strong willed!" she cried. "Is it only the people on the earth who are to be made happy? What about me? Now look at this fruit. From now on, when people see it they will call it crab apple, the sour fruit, and no one will make use of it except the game animals."

"You are putting too much energy into making life difficult for your grandchildren, the human beings," Skyholder replied. "We will go no further now. Perhaps it would be better if you did not see all the things that I have planted, and the game animals."

"Flint and I will go home now," she said, "but things between us need to be settled. When I return, you and I will play a game to see who will be in charge of all the things here on this world. If I win, I will be in charge. And if you win, I will not bother you or interfere in any way in your work."

"Agreed," Skyholder answered.

While they were talking, Flint had been studying the human being which had only recently come to life. "What kind of thing have you done in making this being so well? He appears physically strong."

"The earth is now young and still growing, and it has spiritual power. And the animals are still young, and still growing, and they too have spiritual power. And the human being, too, is still young and still growing, and the human being also has spiritual power," Skyholder replied.

"Yes," Flint responded. "Now I understand. Now my grandmother and I will return home." And they departed.

But when they arrived at the water which separated the island they had visited from their home island, the floating bridge was nowhere in sight.

"What will we do?" Grandmother Blossoms asked. "There's no way to get across."

Flint had a plan. He quickly built a canoe and he and Mature Blossoms crossed the waters to their home island. Then he said, "Now I am going to set about the task of

Gamble for Life

making all kinds of animals, and I am not going to tell my brother anything about it."

He worked quickly and soon he had completed the first one. "Come," he commanded his new creation, "stand up and walk." But the creature was able to only drag its body along and it shortly disappeared. Then Flint took up earth and fashioned another, and again the new creature was unable to stand and walk and it crawled away. "It would appear that this is how things will be," he said to himself, "so I will make many of them and will cause them to go to my brother's island and when they are there they will continually cause trouble." And he continued to make new animals as fast as he could, finishing one and throwing the body aside and beginning another. In a short time they were very numerous, but also most were very ugly.

When he had made many such creatures and they were numerous, Flint gathered them together and said, "Now there is something I want you to do. I want you to go to my brother's island. There are many good things to eat over there, and it does not matter to me if you eat everything you find there."

Some of these animals were fierce and the whole of them plunged into the water and made their way to Skyholder's island. Skyholder already sensed the approach of these animals and he thought, "it wouldn't be good for these animals to mix with the animals I have created," and then he drove all of Flint's animals back across the water. He then followed them and herded them back to the mountain and into the cave where Flint had once imprisoned all the animals. Then he rolled the great rock over the opening of the cave.

"I should consider what I will do if Flint finds out that I have trapped all his animals in the cave," he thought. Then he departed for home.

Gamble for Life

When he arrived, he regarded the work he had done in completing the human being. "I think the work I have done in completing the human being is not finished," he thought. "He appears lonely, so I will create another and then there will be a pair." Then he took up earth and formed the body of a female human being and he took a portion of his own life and placed it in the body he had formed and also a portion of his mind and placed it in the head of her body. He took a portion of his own blood and placed it in her body, then he breathed his own breath into her and she came to life. "Now," he said, "you must stand erect."

As soon as she stood erect, he said, "I have created all the things of this earth," and then he summoned the male human being to their presence. "I have completed both your bodies, and it is my plan that you two shall marry. It will be through hard work that you who have married will have peaceful minds." And then he turned to the male human. "And it will be by your hard work that you will have peaceful minds. So do not ever distress her mind."

He turned again to the female human being, Awenhaniyonda (Inseparable Flower). "It is only through hard work that your partner will continue to have a vigorous life. And it will come to pass that you will see the suffering that happens when a human being takes form inside your body. You will tend the fire, and he who has become your helper in all things will have a peaceful mind."

"Future generations of human beings will take the same shape as you two, and there will be numerous humans who will inhabit the earth. Each of you will individually live a different number of days on the earth, and you will be united in marriage during your natural lives."

"Now I have mixed together your minds and your blood, and you will see human beings take shape through your two

Gamble for Life

bodies. By your minds and your blood you will be bound together, and it is my wish that you two married people will have one mind at all times. Do not either of you distress the other's mind during the days which are yours. Only death will separate you, and only for the difference in the number of days you have."

"It will continue to be this way. Your coming generations will continue to grow up and marry. They will marry only one person. It will continue to be so for as long as the earth shall last. Now I have completed all things."

Soon Flint discovered that the fierce animals he had created were nowhere to be found. He looked over the entire island, and then he went to the other island, but still he found nothing. Finally, he arrived at the lodge of his brother.

"You must know that the animals I have created have come to your island. I cannot find them, so I came here to search.

"You should search over the whole island," Skyholder said, "and since you alone can recognize them when you see them, perhaps you can find them here on this island."

Flint scoured the island and saw many animals of many types, but none of those he had created. Suddenly he came across the two human beings, and he said, "What are you doing here?"

"We have been left here by the one who created us," came the reply.

Flint returned to his brother's lodge. "I didn't find the creatures I sought. I did find the two human beings, a male and a female. When I asked them what they were doing here, they said they had been left by the one who created them. And there is another matter. The animals I completed have disappeared."

Skyholder pointed to the distance. "Who made the

Gamble for Life

mountain? And who made the cavern underneath it?"

Flint immediately understood that his earlier deed, when he had hidden the animals in the cavern, had been reversed and he was the victim of his own plan. He was now embarrassed and became agitated. "I believe," he said, "the animals have made it so."

"If the animals have this much power," Skyholder replied, "and I can believe they made a cavern in the earth, then they are like those who are lost and are living there now."

"Let's go and see," Flint said.

In a short time they arrived at the mountain and the rock which blocked the entrance to the great cavern. "This is the place the animals have their cavern," Skyholder announced. They took the rock and threw it aside. Flint was astonished to see that the only animals which came forth were the monsters he had fashioned. These came forth, some crawling, others dragging their bodies and showing their fierce tempers, snarling and baring their teeth.

"I don't think it would be good if these creatures were to mingle with human beings," Skyholder proposed. "Should the human beings see them, perhaps the humans would die. It would be better if these creatures continue to abide here in this cavern inside the earth."

"There are other beings, even larger than these, which are probably somewhere in the cavern. Perhaps they shall stay there," Flint replied. Then he replaced the rock over the entrance to the cavern. "If they need to come out, they will find their own way. Now that this matter is completed, let us go to our grandmother's lodge." When they arrived, Flint spoke. "Grandmother, everything is accomplished. Now it is up to you. What do you want?"

The old woman said, "My daughter's head is giving

Gamble for Life

me distress. It has been a long time that her head has been hanging here at this lodge. I think her head should be fastened up high so that human beings who travel about here can see it and it will remind them of what has happened. Then my mind will be at rest."

"We should cause her to come to life again," Skyholder said. "We shall place her in the sky and she will be assigned a duty. When darkness comes, she will cause there to be light. It will be her duty to give off heat to protect the earth from becoming too cold during the night and in that way she will help support all the life on the earth. She shall cause all the beings, the animals and the human beings, to be at peace when it is night time. She will command respect for all time, and the human beings who will live on the earth shall use her to measure time and they will govern themselves thereby."

Now Flint spoke. "I cannot agree to all of that. I do agree that she should be placed up high, but high in a tree, not in the sky. It would be enough that human beings would look at her from time to time. If anyone or anything should try to destroy her, I would myself defend her."

"All of this will come to pass as pleases you two, but I must remark that the way you have arranged this will be but of little benefit to anyone."

"There is another matter which needs attention. You, grandmother, have struck my door post with a stick and thus issued a challenge that we should gamble. You said that you and I will play and that whoever wins will prevail over all that exists on the earth. Now I am ready. You had said, 'in ten days we shall play.'"

"I am ready," Mature Blossoms replied. "Keep watch, for soon I shall arrive at your lodge."

Then Skyholder returned to his lodge and he

Gamble for Life

assembled the people who lived there and he said, "Now we are approaching a crisis. The Grandmother has challenged me to a gambling game. If she wins, she will cause everything that grows that supports you and the animals to cease to exist. If I win, everything that exists here on the earth will continue to live and that will be good, but it will be only temporary. Eventually their forces seek to ruin all of my works.

"What will happen is that two things will take place in the coming days. It will be hot on the earth for a season, and during that time all the plants that grow here will mature. And it will grow cold for a season, and the water will grow hard. Then again it will become mellow, and the snow will melt, and things will once again grow and therefore it will result in good that there shall be two seasons in the coming days."

"Another good thing is that there will be an orb of light at night, a nighttime sun, and it represents my mother, your Grandmother. She will aid our Elder Brother, the daytime sun. The people on the earth will continue to hold respect for these two. And the nighttime sun will continue to shrink and customarily will disappear during three nights, and then will grow again in the coming days."

Then he sat at the entrance to his lodge and awaited his grandmother. Soon she and Flint arrived, and Skyholder announced, "Ah, Mature Blossoms and my brother Flint, now you have come to take everything I have fashioned.

"And you two human beings, you are witnesses to this struggle, and you will tell your descendants of what has happened here for as long as the earth exists. In the future your descendants will see many things, and Flint will do many abnormal things and your descendants will see many fearful things."

Then the grandmother said, "So it shall come to pass. I have brought my own bowl and pieces and we will use

Gamble for Life

these," and she produced a wooden bowl with six peach stones. One side of each of the peach stones was dark, the other light, and the game required five of one color to score one, a field of six of one color to score five.

"You will use your pieces and I will use my own. We will each throw the bowl once, and you will be satisfied with the outcome. Perhaps the good luck will fall to you, or perhaps it will fall to me."

"Are you ready?" the grandmother asked.

"I will get my pieces," he said.

He started back toward his lodge and as he walked he turned and he said "come with me, you chickadees, six of you." The chickadees flocked to him. "The grandmother and I are going to bet, and I need your assistance. We are going to play to three points. We will bet the plants in the first round, the animals in the second, and the human beings in the third. Now I will use your heads."

At this they sang and they perched themselves along his body and he beheaded them. Then he returned to his grandmother and said, "Let us begin. We will each throw the bowl once."

"I will throw first," the old woman said and then she threw, but her throw came out poorly and she scored no points.

"Take your pieces out. It is my turn," Skyholder rejoined. Then he put his pieces in the bowl and the pieces acted as though they were alive as they raced about the inside and he said, "Listen, you whose bodies I have formed, bring out all your power so that we will win and all will continue to live," and he shook the bowl. Now there was a loud voice, and the sounds of the various animal cries, and all the things that grow on the earth and these voices raised a great clamor. The pieces sang and then they flew up high into the air and

Gamble for Life

out of sight, and the sound went with them. Now Skyholder and his grandmother each put out all their power and he cried out "Let there become a perfect score!" and she cried "pshaw!," "Let there be nothing!"

After a time they heard sounds of birds coming in the distance and now they were coming downward and they made tremendous noises. Suddenly they landed in the bowl and he shouted "Let there be a perfect score!" and she shouted, "Let there be no score!"and for a long time the pits rolled around in the bowl. Then they became still, and all turned up black. Skyholder had won five points and the game.

"I have rolled a perfect score," Skyholder rejoiced, "and have answered your challenge. For a long time you have been scheming to strip from me all that I have completed. Now the matter is settled. It will come to pass that the humans who have newly come to life shall come into control of the earth, and the memory of this will pass to future generations of humans. When they tell of this, your name will be She, the Ancient One, the Grandmother. Now it has happened that everything is taken from you. You will be remembered, and those who inhabit the earth will tell of you."

Then he said, "Now as to you two, your lives are still in your infancy. You, male person, you shall be known as Odendonni"a -- Youngtree. And the one who is with you, she shall be Awenhaniyonda -- Inseparable Flower. Such shall be your names, and your lives shall endure as long as the earth exists. Your names signify that there are always growing bushes and growing trees and grasses with flowers. So it will be forever. Always new things will be coming to life."

"Now we must give thanks that we have triumphed for all time and can continue to be peacefully contented. You, Youngtree, will be the first to offer thanksgiving. You will cry out three times and all will repeat your words, and that will

Gamble for Life

signify that now we are all happy. This is what will happen for all time, for whatever reasons people will rejoice."

Now Youngtree cried out three times and he repeated it three times. The sounds were extremely loud, and all the various animals followed his voice. All cried out.

"There is one more matter," Skyholder continued. "Flint, you and your grandmother must at once return to me the head of my deceased mother. Now I am in charge of everything."

"I have not yet given up the head," Flint answered. "So I do not agree that you have won the right to decide everything. You must destroy all my powers before that happens."

"I have not done what I have done merely to be doing things differently. I have done these things so that all of us should have contented minds," Skyholder, the Master Of Life, replied.

Then the old woman said, "It would not be good if Flint would challenge you." To Flint she continued, "All that you and I would usually decide about has been lost. Now we will go home."

Gamble for Life

FIVE
GRANDMOTHER

    In time the two humans gave birth to children and they traveled about with their family. At that time Skyholder said to them, "I have decided how you can help me. I want to possess the head of my mother. I want you to get it and bring it to me. You will fully prepare yourself. First, get red willow and prepare a medicine that can purify your bodies. Use the medicine three times before sunrise for three days. Then we will start.

    "We will divide the work among us. Youngtree, you will go about this island and if you see the horn of a deer lying on the ground you will place it up high. Next, if you see a flint lying on the ground, place it up high.

    "Do this carefully and thoroughly. Do not leave any lying on the ground. If you do this as I have instructed, we will survive and will be able to ward off Flint's powers. Once we retrieve the head, he will be able to follow us back, so I will also go to his island. I will then go about his island and all the antler I find I will place up high, and also the flint."

    "When Flint sees all the flint and horn up high, he will believe that everyone has turned against him. When

Grandmother

that happens, he will become silent and will seat himself in the lodge. So all this work must be done by the time I return." Youngtree set out on his assignment.

Skyholder went to Flint's island. When he arrived there, he went all over. Wherever he found flint or horn, he placed these up high off the ground. When he was finished, he searched the island until he found a certain tree. The head he sought was fastened at the top of this tree, and he saw that nearby the tree Flint waited in ambush.

Now Skyholder turned to leave and he went toward a mountain in the distance. Soon, unexpectedly, he came across a being shaped similar to a human being who said, "Where did you come from?"

"In the distance there is an island. I am going about examining the world. And you," Shyholder replied. "Where did you come from?"

"I come from the direction of the setting sun, and I too am examining the world. I own this world, I have completed everything here."

"What is your name?" Skyholder asked.

"I am called Hadu'i', The Face. And you?"

"I am called Skyholder. I finished the bodies of the human beings who walk on the earth. I would like very much to see how much power you have since you continue to say that you have completed the earth as it is."

Face carried in his hand a great turtle rattle and now he began to shake it and it made a great noise. All the animals around were very frightened at this demonstration.

"That's not enough," Skyholder said. "To prove the things you say, I would like to see you move that mountain in the distance. Bring it here."

"That wouldn't prove anything." Then, he continued. "All right. Let's face away from the mountain." When they were both facing away from the mountain, Face

Grandmother

said, "Mountain, come here! Come to where we stand, at our backs." Then he addressed Skyholder, saying "You and I will stop breathing as long as we can hold our breaths."

So they stopped breathing. When they had held their breaths as long as they could, Face said, "Come, let us turn around again." When they turned around they saw that the mountain had moved but slightly.

"It's obvious you can't move the mountain," Skyholder said. "That means it is not you who have created the earth. Now I will try to move it. If the mountain moves at my command it will be proof that it is I who have created all. So let's turn around again."

The two once again faced away from the mountain, and Skyholder said, "Mountain, come here to our backs." Then he addressed Face, saying "Let us hold our breaths. The contest will be over at the length of time you can hold your breath. Then I will say 'now!' Do not look until then."

The two were quiet while they held their breaths and after a time Face was aware that something grazed his back. Then he thought, "I must see what is happening," and he quickly turned around. As he did so, his face struck the mountain ledge. Just then Skyholder announced, "Let's turn around again." At that moment he noticed that Face's nose had become twisted, and also his mouth and he said, "Listen. It is I who have completed all on this earth. But what has happened to you? Something has changed your appearance."

"It is true you have great power," Hadu'i' replied, "and were able to move the mountain from afar and that because of your power this has happened to me. I thought I would see what it was that had touched my shoulder, and when I turned around my face struck the mountain. Then I understood that it was you who finished the earth, because you were able to control the mountain."

Grandmother

"I therefore will humble myself. I will be able to help you with the humans who are about to settle on the earth. I can aid them. Soon these human beings will be experiencing visions.

"Power resides in me, and I have spread this power throughout the earth. I was the first to wander to and fro about the earth, and soon humans will experience visions as they go about the earth. It will happen that people will become ill and their faces will be contorted as mine is, and their bodies, and sometimes they will encounter bad medicine. If people make a wooden form patterned after my face, it may be possible that I can help human beings who are ill to recover. This is how I will help you with the things you have completed among human beings.

"When people are cured in this way, they will continue to be contented. This is what will be in the future and I am going to say something more. I believe I can help the people you have formed. I also believe that Flint, who hates your intentions, will go to any length to destroy your work, and that people shall become ill and shall suffer mental anguish and that his plans are to put an end to the days of human beings.

"I will try ceaselessly to help human beings and will continue to drive away illness so that humans may have some remaining days. They will remember me because I help them and they will address me as 'My Dear Grandfather', and when, as a group they are thinking of me, they will address me as 'Our Dear Grandfather.' And I will also address them as 'My Dear Grandchildren,' when I direct my words to the people who go about on the earth. Now there is nothing that would prevent them from making something that will resemble me.

"It will be possible that from a certain tree which is especially hardy, and which is called the white pine, that

Grandmother

people shall make the masks which will resemble my face today. They will use that as a means to call on me so that I may repeatedly blow upon one who is ill. There is nothing wrong with a human being imitating me for this purpose. Let them cover their face with the mask and go to the lodges of the people and there the society of the Face must impersonate me.

"As soon as they arrive the members of the society must blow air repeatedly on the person who is ill, and it will be just as if it is I who had blown on them repeatedly. People will bring native tobacco. When one speaks to me, one customarily will hold native tobacco in their hand. At that time it is necessary that people will throw the tobacco on the fire. I will inhale the smoke that rises, and it will be custom that ashes will be taken from the fire and will be used to blow repeatedly over the entire body of the person who is sick. Then, at that time, the disease or affliction will go away or be eased.

"Next, when one calls upon me, one should have prepared a favorite of mine, a kettle of parched corn meal mush. This will continue in this fashion no matter what time of year."

Then Skyholder spoke, saying "Now you have settled the matter of your duties on the earth." Then the two parted.

Skyholder then went home where he spoke to Youngtree. "I have returned. Now everything is arranged. Let's go to retrieve the head of my mother."

"I have done everything you requested, and I am ready."

Skyholder made a canoe and he said, "Everyone who has faith that they will not fail, even if we are pursued, come with us." A number of beings emerged from the forest including Fox who said, "I will volunteer."

Grandmother

"What can you do?" Skyholder asked.

"I will take up the head when it falls to the ground and I will run with it."And in a short time Fisher arrived. Fisher said, "I will take the head from Fox and will fly swiftly over the water. No one will catch me." Skyholder responded and said, "Your plan will not succeed."

Then another came forth and his name was Beaver. "I will also help," he said.

"And how can you help us?"

"When we arrive there, I will stay with the canoe. If it becomes necessary, I can cut down the tree."

"Now here we have someone who can help us," Skyholder said. And Fox and Fisher said, "We will go, too. We will paddle the canoe." And they all departed.

When they arrived, Skyholder and Youngtree stood at the top at the bank, and Beaver stayed with the canoe. "If you need me," Beaver said, "call out my name and I'll be there." Fisher also ascended the bank and he said, "I will wait here and if I am needed, call out my name and I'll appear."

Now Skyholder and Youngtree departed. Soon they came to Flint's lodge. When they arrived, no one was present and Youngtree said, "I will try to climb to the top of the tree to retrieve the head." Then he began to climb, but halfway he was forced back down. "I am unable to climb it," he said.

"Ah," said Skyholder, "I see that I have made a mistake. It appears that something is lacking in your body. I never thought you would need to climb trees or I would have completed your feet. You have no instep. Hold up your foot."

Youngtree held up his foot and Skyholder took hold of it and pressed the middle part inward. "Now I have completed this," Skyholder said, "now climb the tree. In a

Grandmother

short time those two will arrive and I don't think we have time to do what we are trying to do."

Youngtree quickly climbed it. He ascended quickly and easily and when he arrived at the top he quickly took the head. Then, carrying the head, he began to descend, but as he did so he slipped and his descent was rapid and clumsy, tearing branches and stripping the bark. "I came down so quickly," he said, "and stripped the bark and the tree just shines."

"They will tell this story for a long time," Skyholder said. "They will name this the sycamore tree."

At that instant, Flint and his grandmother appeared. The grandmother immediately looked at the tree and saw that the head was gone. At once she shouted and she cried, "They have taken the head from us. Get moving!"

All kinds of animals cried out in a great noise. Flint now understood what had taken place and he said, "Something is going to happen because an attempt is being made to kill me. Deer horns and flint stones have been placed up high everywhere, and so I can't do anything. You will have to get the head back. Follow them!"

The grandmother ran swiftly to the tree. There she saw the footprints of the human being heading into the west. Now she ran swiftly in that direction, following the trail of Skyholder and his friends. They could hear her following them as she shouted, "Bring back the head!"

At that time Fox said, "Give it to me. I am very fast and she won't catch me." And Youngtree replied, "I think I had better not give it to you. I don't trust you."

Then Black Squirrel said, "Let me have it. I'll carry it across the tops of the trees. She won't get the head back."

"If it becomes necessary, you will have it," Youngtree said.

In a short time Youngtree became aware that the old

Grandmother

woman was gaining on him. He put all his strength to running. Overhead, in the trees, Black Squirrel and Fisher raced through the treetops, doing all they could to keep up with Youngtree. Although they had gone a long ways, the old woman kept getting closer.

"Be brave," Skyholder said. "Use all your strength," and both continued to run as fast as they could. They shortly arrived at the place where Beaver waited in the canoe and they climbed in and Skyholder said, "It is time that all of you should help us. Youngtree, you must paddle and steer." At that moment Otter came out of the water and climbed in the canoe. "I will paddle," he said. Muskrat climbed aboard, and he also paddled. Now they turned their canoe around and paddled as hard as they could.

In an instant the old woman appeared on the shore and they could see that she was very angry.

"Youngtree," she cried, "Give me back what you have taken. Give me the head!" But Youngtree did not reply. Then she said, "Beaver, have pity on me. You are steering. Bring it back here!" But Beaver made no reply. Then she cried, "Oh Muskrat! Have pity on me. Bring it back." And Muskrat said, "O.K."

Skyholder then spoke to Muskrat, saying "You have become irresponsible in your actions. You should not have replied. Now you will be a humble being on the earth and at all times you will go along the edge of the waters." Then they cast Muskrat overboard.

Then Otter became frightened and said, "I too will take myself out of the canoe." Skyholder said "That is up to you. You didn't have to come. In the future and for all time you will continue to be shy and you will hide yourself. You will go back and forth in the depths of the waters." Then Otter went overboard.

In a moment they had lost sight of the old woman,

Grandmother

and she went about weeping and crying out.

When they arrived at the place from which they had started, Skyholder spoke to Beaver, saying, "You were a great help. In the future you will have a great deal of power. You will be able to control the flow of waters. Indeed, you will have the power to decide if you want to make earth for yourself, or if you want to dam up the water for yourself, and it will come about exactly as you plan."

"I will now make my mother's flesh whole again." And then he made it over again, using the air. When he finished, she stood before them, her body restored. Skyholder continued, "Your body and your powers have become whole again. My brother caused ruin to befall you as the first victim on the earth. He is continuing to cause ruin, and will do so as long as the earth endures."

"My mother, it is my plan that you will have a duty. You will attend to the earth, and also the grasses, and the grown clumps of bushes, and the forests of all kinds of trees and the many other things that habitually grow here -- humans and animals."

"The seasons will change and Elder Brother Sun will cause the earth to become warm and when this happens it will be Springtime. Then the various vegetation will begin to grow until they are mature and then it will become cold again. You and Elder Brother will assist each other. When it becomes dark on the earth, you will cause it to be hot and will cause there to be light and will cause the dew to fall. You will continue to assist your grandchildren, the human beings."

Then he took red willow and he scraped off the bark. "Now you will depart. Now the people will continue to say of you that they will see you newly again, that you slowly continue to draw nearer, and you will slowly increase in size night after night. When you rise, your form will be complete

Grandmother

and full. As you continue to move along night after night your form will grow less until you return to the place from which you depart. The length of time of your path shall be constant, and because of this the people will forever hold you in high esteem.

"Now you understand your duties and the matter is completed. You and the Sun share the responsibility. When they who dwell on the earth will address their words to you, they will say 'O Sun, our Elder Brother, the Great War Chief,' and when they address their words to you they will say 'O Our Grandmother Moon.' I have left here the principle thing they will use when they address you, the native tobacco.

"Whenever the people think of the skyworld, they must take up the tobacco and hold it in their hands and throw it into the fire. The smoke will become their word. It will continue to be so for as long as the earth exists. Now, for myself, I employ that which first grew on the earth, the red willow. I am now ready to use that for you, for now you will go to the place you have been assigned."

Then he took the red willow and cast it on the fire and he said, "Throw yourself onto the fire, the smoke is rising!" And she threw herself onto the fire and her body rose into the air with the smoke.

"Now, human beings, you must watch and take note of what has taken place. Inseparable Flower, you will notice a change will come over your life and as you see the moon become new it will be a sign that the life you carry has become renewed and this will start the formation of new human beings. This will begin the first time you see the Moon, your Grandmother. And her power will extend in this way to all the things that grow, and the animals, and all the human beings.

At that time Youngtree and his wife, Inseparable

Grandmother

Flower, carefully observed the moon and after three nights Inseparable Flower was surprised that a change came over her. "Now that which was promised has happened," she said. Youngtree was surprised to see the moon present in the western sky. "Let me go and tell the one who made our bodies." And she went to Skyholder and related that which had happened.

"Now this matter is completed. From now forward, the moon and the life of human beings will go together. And human beings shall associate the two with the birth of human beings. Now I will go to travel about, and you two are free to travel about. You will learn of my fate, for when my brother and I meet, we will certainly have a great disagreement.

"When beasts and ugly animals appear, you will know that this has happened, for my brother will drive such beasts from the cavern where they now abide. Such beasts will abuse, slaughter, and eat the flesh of things here. When you see this happen, you will know we two brothers have disagreed.

"If this happens, I will try to move my grandmother elsewhere, and I will try to bring about a peaceful solution. Then, of course, he and I will be left alone. I think it would be desirable, should this happen, that he and I should go elsewhere for there would be a lot of destruction should we engage each other here."

Then he left and he went to the island of his brother. The island was inhabited by all manner of fierce and ugly creatures. He arrived at his grandmother's lodge to learn that Flint was not home.

"I have come to find you, grandmother. It is time that you go to another place."

"I cannot go. Flint would not be pleased if he returns and finds me gone."

Grandmother

"You must go anyway. Go to my lodge and wait for me to return. I will talk to Flint and explain that you have gone."

"I cannot go because he will not know where I have gone," the grandmother answered. "His mind is already troubled because someone has stolen the head of the mother of you two."

"Look into the distance," Skyholder replied. "The one you are talking about is looking this way."

She turned to look just as the moon arose, its rays bursting through the forest.

"It is true," she said, "it is the mother of you two. Now my mind has become once again positive."

"Go now," he said. "It will not be long before you will go upward again. You will have a duty to perform and you will assist her. There is still one who is absent who should attend to things on the earth. I do not desire to spoil anything my brother has done. He and I will not argue about anything. It does not matter that I did not make everything."

"It would make me happy if you and your brother did agree," the grandmother said.

"I would also like that. But if it's not possible, then things here will change."

Now the grandmother began her journey. Soon she arrived at the Skyholder's island and she looked for Youngtree and Inseparable Flower but she couldn't find them. When she arrived at Skyholder's lodge, no one was there. She waited. Soon the two humans returned and she said, "I have arrived. I don't know what happened after I left, but Flint was not home and Skyholder awaits him. I don't know what will happen when Flint returns. Flint is very angry because someone has stolen the Head. He had it fastened up high, but someone took it."

Youngtree said, "Grandmother, continue to have

Grandmother

positive thoughts. His mother has a duty to perform. Look there, in the sky where you see an orb of light."

Now she looked at it and said, "Yes. It is true. It is she who is looking at us." And she was satisfied.

Skyholder waited at the lodge of his grandmother but after several days he became concerned because Flint did not return. Then Skyholder went looking for him. He traveled all over the island, but he couldn't find him anywhere. He did find two male human beings going about. When he approached them he said, "have you seen the owner of Flint's lodge?"

"He was here just a moment ago," one of them answered. "Moreover, presumably it was he who caused the orb of light which now appears in the nighttime sky."

Skyholder explained to them that it was he, Skyholder, who had caused the moon to cross the sky, and he instructed them as he had instructed Youngtree and Inseparable Flower. Then he continued on his search. As he approached his brother's lodge, he saw a pile of flint stones and he took these and carried them into the lodge. He placed these stones at the spot where Flint usually sat, and as he turned to leave, Flint appeared.

"No one is home," Skyholder announced.

"Isn't my grandmother here? She was here when I left."

"Let's go inside. You'll see no one is home."

Once inside Flint saw that she was not present, then he noticed that flint stones had been arranged at the place he customarily sat. At this, he turned to go out in despair. "Now I can see that my grandmother has turned against me," he said. "She doesn't care that someone might take me prisoner, or might kill me. Now I must defend myself. I must take control of everything!"

"Why would you think everyone has turned against

Grandmother

you?" Skyholder asked. "I don't think so. Personally, I would rather help you. I hope there will be peace in this world and in the world above."

"Then why would someone have arranged these things -- the horn and flint -- which have the power to destroy me? Look at the place where I usually sit. Someone has put several things there that can kill me. No matter where I go I see things which are dangerous to me affixed in a way that I could be injured. That is why someone has carried away our mother's head and our grandmother is gone.

"Now I can't do anything else. Someone is trying to kill me and I must defend myself. No one can help me, and if I am to live, I can help no one. And I will have pity on no one. I will be happy only when I am in control of everything."

"I don't know what you're talking about," Skyholder replied. "There is no problem. Everything is peaceful."

"I don't like it that all people look to you for everything. No one dislikes you. That is what I mean. I will be pleased only when I control everything and that includes how people think about you. When I am successful, all people will dislike you!"

"It should be clear. There is nothing wrong. No one is hostile to you."

"I have lost everything," Flint cried. "My grand-mother and my mother are gone. I will not change my mind."

"I don't understand why you are so angry," Skyholder said. "It was you who killed our mother. Even so, she has come to life again, and now she will live forever, and even that makes you unhappy. Because it was you who killed her, it will not be possible for you to see her up close. It will be a custom for all time that one who murders a

Grandmother

human being will not be forgiven."

At this moment, Flint became very angry. "Let us go outside and settle this matter!" he demanded. The two went outdoors.

"All those things whose bodies I have formed shall continue to devour those things whose bodies I did not form," Flint said. "I call upon the Daylight and the Darkness and the waters to help me with their powers to destroy those things I did not create. Even the power of the mind will be used to help destroy those beings I did not create."

"What you are doing is wrong. You are planning to bring about the destruction of humankind and before you do that, you must destroy me," Skyholder said.

"I have already determined that you and I must fight if you don't like my plan."

"You have turned your thoughts into an accusation against me," Skyholder responded. "What do you want us to do?"

"You will use your powers in combat," Flint replied, "and I will use mine."

"I will not trick you. I will use my power, the power of daylight. And I will use the mountain."

"I will use darkness," Flint boasted, "and it is in darkness that we will enter into combat." Then he jumped forward, waving in his hand the flint-tipped arrow. "Already I have killed one person, and I will use my arrow to kill another."

Skyholder quickly took hold of the arrow and the two struggled for it. Then there arose a loud sound, and it became cloudy, and the wind grew in power. Now Skyholder let go of the arrow and before Flint could move he took hold of the mountain and cast it over the place where Flint had stood. In a moment Flint broke free and fled and Skyholder pursued him.

Grandmother

Now the two circled around the island repeatedly. Skyholder repeatedly took up the mountain and cast it over Flint, and repeatedly Flint was covered over but then emerged. Then it happened that several mountains were joined together. Flint threw back rocks. Skyholder caught the rocks and threw them back again and after a while the mountain became covered with rocks. While this battle raged the animals hid themselves, and some of them fled.

Flint repeatedly tried to hide in the mountains, but each time he would be discovered. Then Skyholder called on Earthquake, saying, "Now is the time you should help me!"

At that time great sounds were heard over the earth and the earth's movements increased in force until the world began to quake in a violent way.

"That is enough!," Flint cried. "You have demonstrated your powers. I surrender. You have the power, and now I will remain quiet. All I will retain is my mind."

"So be it, but I don't think you should remain in this place. You should go to a different world."

"I would agree to that if you will agree that we shall not be far apart," Flint said.

"Then you will continue to exist here as long as you do nothing wrong. If you do something wrong, I will be forced to imprison your body."

"I have surrendered. I don't know what will happen if there is a next time. But first, I would like permission to visit my home."

"That is acceptable, but only until I have finished the rest of my work. I am not satisfied with that which takes place during the nighttime. Whenever the moon is invisible, the darkness becomes complete. I will create stars to aid the moon so that there will be light. And I will create one which will bring the day, which we will call Morning Star. When

Grandmother

you see the large star, then the night will change, and the two will exchange themselves, and a new daylight will be on the earth. When you see the large star, go to my lodge. I will be expecting you."

When Skyholder arrived the grandmother asked, "What happened? There was lightning all night. When the moon rose, the earth shook. I thought one of you must have been destroyed."

"The argument between us is settled. One of us was almost killed, but now that is behind us. Now nothing is wrong, and we are both alive.

"You have accomplished all that you were required to do here on the earth, and now you will go home once again, back to the place you came from. And you will have the same body when you arrive there as you had then. You will go directly to the place where you first acquired the power of thought. At the end of ten days, unless my brother and I disagree, we also will return there."

Then he went out and took red willow and scraped the bark from them. He threw the bark on the fire and as the smoke rose he said, "Grandmother, throw yourself on this and begin your return journey. When I arrive at the place you are going, I will create the rains so that the earth will continuously be renewed." And the grandmother threw herself into the smoke and ascended to the sky.

Then Skyholder turned to Youngtree and Inseparable Flower and said, "Now you are seeing the grandmother depart for her home in the sky world. Now in the future only the word and the thoughts of the mind will be able to ascend to the sky world. They will be carried upward with the smoke from the native tobacco which will be cast on the fire. As the smoke rises, one shall speak and the words will join with the smoke and go on high. It will be as good as if the person who speaks the word were able to ascend

Grandmother

himself, but from now forward, no persons will be able to ascend in the smoke."

"Now I will tell you that I will make stars to be placed in the visible sky. From now on and into the future, those who have been upright people and who have done no wrong, when they have lived the allotted days of their lives, will ascend to the sky world and will join and mingle with the body of stars. So long as the earth shall continue to exist, the stars will continue to increase in number. There will come a time when there will be no one on the earth who will be able to count all the stars in the sky. And to some of the animals, when they have accomplished their duties on earth, it will be possible that they, too, will become visible as stars in the sky.

Now he left and he went to the underwater lodge of De'hao''hwendjyawa'k'ho'' (He Holds the Earth by His Hands). "I have come here," he began, "because there are things which should be created. First, I think I should make a new star, one which will be called T'hende''hawit''ha' (He Brings The Morning With Him). No one on the earth has ever yet seen you. You should become the one who brings the day. Then you would show yourself, and people would see you at the place where daylight is formed. The reason it should be so is that you provided all the thoughts that inspired the whole of my work."

"This is all correct," the old man said. "You have done everything which needed to be done. Now I will tell you, when your brother comes, you two must keep together, and you must constantly watch him. When you are ready to leave the earth, do not consent to his request to stay behind. He continues to desire revenge and to destroy all that you have created here. You must insist that you two depart together.

"There will be a pathway visible in the night sky and

Grandmother

it will be plain that your two minds differ and the path will be divided. The people on the earth, when it is nighttime and cloudless, will always be able to see this path."

"I will act on this advice," Skyholder said, "and now I turn over to you the responsibility that when the day will be dawning you will show yourself for a short time. Then the human beings will have an opportunity to see you. You will be the first, each day, to see all I have created. Next, the sun will attend to all I have created as long as he will cause it to be light. The sun and moon will follow one another. When it becomes dark, the moon will appear. There will not at any time be an interval, a period when none of the sky world beings is in attendance, for as long as the earth shall last.

"I have invited my brother, and as soon as he sees the Morning Star he will appear at my lodge. Then I will know what he intends to do. At first, I thought it would be wise if I were to destroy all the things he has created, for some of them have the power to inflict injury and destruction on my work. They can destroy the beings I have created and cause no end of havoc. Some of them are so powerful that just the sight of them can cause destruction. Thus it will be that they will remain forever inside the mountains. Only at the end of time, when my works will decline, will they be able to leave the interior of the earth.

"So now I will appoint those beings who will have the duty of attending to the needs of the earth so that the days and nights will continue to be renewed. And they will also be responsible that the streams of waters will always be renewed and will never fail, and they shall cleanse the earth. And it will be they who will keep the fierce creatures confined in the earth. And so, too, the human beings will be in the habit of addressing Hadiwennodadie's' -- The Thunderers. The Thunderers will be in the habit of coming

Grandmother

from the west and they will continue to have power as long as the earth shall exist.

And the Ancient One said, "Your ideas are good. Hopefully, the human beings will not be long disturbed when they hear their voices when they come and cause the sky to resound."

"Now I am going to my home," Skyholder said.

When he arrived at his lodge, Youngtree and Inseparable Flower were present. "Now, for the first time, you will see a star which will signal the coming daylight," Skyholder announced. "And soon Flint will return. His presence signals a crisis for us. Listen to what he says."

Soon Flint arrived and he said, "I promised that when I saw the star, I would come. I am here."

"Now you and I must settle our differences," Skyholder announced. "First I will ask a question and you will answer and Youngtree and Inseparable Flower will hear your answer. What I want is your consent that all the things whose bodies you have finished will remain in the earth and in the water.

"I would agree to that if you can agree that I can remain here on the earth," Flint replied.

"I don't think so. The reason I have decided to segregate the human beings and all the creatures I have made from those you have created is that you and I are leaving this earth. Now the two of us are ready to depart," Skyholder said.

"I have a last request. I want you and I to travel one more time over the whole Island. When we first arrived, there was nothing. During the time you and I traveled about, we created many things. We should view these accomplishments again so the human beings will be in the habit of telling stories about them and will remember us from time to time," Flint said.

Grandmother

"This can be done," Skyholder agreed.

Grandmother

SIX
JOHE'KOH – THE SUSTAINERS OF LIFE

Then they traveled about. When they returned, Skyholder called Youngtree and Inseparable Flower into his presence. "After I am gone, you will think of me. I have left for you the sacred tobacco. Do not forget to use it when you think of me. I will hear you at once and the same will be true of all those to whom I have commissioned duties. They will hear your words. Nothing will interfere with their ability to see the earth.

"It will come to pass that sometime in the future I will again come to the earth. Now you two must watch carefully because my brother and I will leave footprints and there will be a path which will mark where we have passed, and it will be clearly in view. When nighttime comes, that path will come clearly into view and that will continue to be the path for those who live here. That is the path that they will take when the number of days they have on the earth are at an end. When one follows that path, they will see me personally.

"Now you will continue to pay attention, and you will see that there are voices which come from the west, the Thunder Voices. It will continue to be so until the end of the earth. When you hear their voices from the eastward, it will be a sign to you that the earth is now nearing its end. Do not let your descendants forget.

"Now your brother and I will ascend to the sky. All that you will have as a sign that this has happened is that you will see the pathway above divided. When you see this, you will know that two kinds of mind have come into being in the world above, and on the earth below, and among human beings." And now the two departed homeward.

Not long after they departed, the people heard a loud noise in the sky. The sound traveled from the west to the east and Youngtree said, "You and I have heard the voices of our grandfathers, the Thunder Voices. Let us greet them with a thanksgiving." Then he cast tobacco on the fire.

Soon it became dark and they saw very plainly a pathway across the sky. Youngtree said, "Now you and I have seen all the things that He-Who-Finished-Our-Bodies (the Creator) has done for us. Now you and I have responsibilities, and we will fulfill our duties forever."

Youngtree and Inseparable Flower now began to have children and in a short time there were a number of family lines. And soon there were a great number of people and all knew that Skyholder had promised to return when the people were numerous.

There was, however, absolute silence. There was no ceremony which they should have been performing, and no business they should have attended to. Everything was simply neglected. Things stayed this way for some time when they were surprised to hear that Skyholder had returned. Now many people desired to see him and a great number searched for a long time before they found him.

"I said I would return when there were many families on the earth," Skyholder stated, "and now I have returned. Now it has come to pass that there are many families, but that things are very much neglected. The human beings seem to merely stand around from place to place, and that is why I have returned.

"Now you must pay attention. All of you who live upon the earth share it equally. Now what I am about to give

Johe'koh

you I shall regard as an important matter. What I will leave here on the earth is the Four Ceremonies. You will observe these. From time to time you will assemble in order to give recognition to the things that grow and support your lives.

"You will assemble the first time when you see the season's first fruit and you will take that fruit which you first see to an appointed place. And the whole body of the people must assemble and you will mutually rejoice. And next you will congratulate one another that so many people have seen life renewed, and you will swallow the fruit upon which you live. Then you will mutually congratulate one another and when you have ended, you will give thanks to me.

"I have patterned the Four Ceremonies after the ceremonies which are taking place in the sky world. The pleasure with which the sky world beings celebrate is most important. I wanted it to be such that the ceremonies in the sky world and those on earth were the same.

"The four ceremonies are the O:stowa'gowa (Great Feather Dance,) the Gone'o (Thanksgiving Drum Dance,) the Adonwe (Personal Chant,) and Gane:hwe'go:wa:h, (Bowl Game or Peachstone Game). These shall be carried on at appointed times. The first will be at the end of the season, as soon as all that upon which you live has matured, and will be the Harvest Festival. At that time all the kinds of things upon which you live will be collected. The Great Feather Dance will commence and all people will rejoice. They will think "I am thankful I am alive and in good health and that I have again seen that upon which we live, that I have again seen the ceremony that was ordained for us.

"And next one will say, 'I thank you repeatedly, you who have formed my body, you who dwell in the sky. I am grateful that I can participate in this ceremony you have provided for us."

"Customarily you must perform all the ceremonies.

Johe'koh

You will dance in one direction during these ceremonies. No one will dance in the opposite direction. As you make a circle, the right side of the body will be on the outside. You will dance around the singers, and you will make use of the feather headdress. When the Four Ceremonies are finished, all should be happy.

"Now it will happen the days will change and it will be cold again. Now the Four Ceremonies will again be marked. At that time the animals will deserve special attention. Now it happens that as the seasons change the bodies of the animals become changed and become weaker, and as it becomes cold once again their bodies change and they become new again and the meat becomes fine. It is at this time that people will hunt.

"Now there will be an assembly and it will be called Ganonhwaiwih (the Greatly Prized Ceremony) and then the buildings where you dwell will become important places. You will set your hands to fire, and when ashes are created you will stir them and then you will say, 'I am thankful I am alive and in health.' Now it is time for Ganonhwaiwih. You, Skyholder, who lives in the sky, do continue to listen. Now I give thanks that it has been possible for me to again see the place you have set the ceremony.' Then one will sing and one will dip a paddle into the ashes and one's voice will accompany that action, and all will rejoice. When all who are alive on the earth have rejoiced, all minds will unite. And at that time you will use the white dogs. I will continue to greatly prize that ceremony.

"All the people of the earth, being of my father's clansmen, will attend to my needs. You will sacrifice a certain species of white dog. The white dog shall have no black spot on it. This will symbolize the form of my raiment. When the time comes, he who casts its body on the fire must next cast tobacco into the fire and say, 'Continue to listen. Now you see

Johe'koh

how many people have come to the place to kindle a fire in your honor. Now they have brought you that which you prize, the white dog. Now the thing you prize is sent to you. Now they thank you repeatedly that it was still possible for so many to see the ceremony you have designed for us. We ask that you send us again the animals you have provided for us. And we ask that all the things you planted here for us to live on continue to provide for us. Now another, we ask that you continue to allow the births of more infants so that they should come forth on the earth, so that your mind can be fulfilled. Now we are using the tobacco. All those assembled here turn their faces toward you with a single voice.

"'Now there is the first thing. To you our Mother Earth upon whom we stand we give thanks. Now we encourage you to have a strong mind so that we should continue to think in peace day after day and night after night.

"'Now another thing. You, our Elder Brother Sun, continue to listen. Those who live on the earth have made preparations to thank you with one voice. They have sent encouragement that your mind will remain firm and you will continue to do your duty as determined by He-Who- Created-Our-Bodies (the Creator).

"And there is another, our Grandmother Moon, and also the Stars in the sky. Those who remain alive have made preparations to thank you in one voice. And they have assembled to encourage you to remain fixed in your minds that you will continue in your duties.

"And there is another to which we direct our attention and it is our Grandfathers the Thunders whose voices come from the west and who are appointed to protect us day after day and night after night. Everyone who remains alive has made preparations to thank you repeatedly and with one voice. They encourage your minds to continue with that to which you were appointed by he who made our bodies.

Johe'koh

"Now there are others who must be acknowledged. We mention those who have duties on the earth -- the grasses that grow, the shrubs, the growing trees, the springs of water, the wind, the daytime, the night time, and the several stars fixed on the sky.

"And another. You, Skyholder, continue to listen. The ceremony will be performed by we who are living on the earth. You will see that when the ceremony starts, you will be the principle beneficiary. You will be thanked repeatedly. Tomorrow the Great Feather Dance will start, and on the day after tomorrow we will start the Thanksgiving (Drum) Dance, and they will select someone who will give thanks repeatedly. He will begin with all those things which are contained on the earth which give satisfaction to people's minds.

"And the next day, the Ceremony of Chanting, Adonwa, will start. This ceremony rests entirely with the individual. The individual will repeatedly give thanks.

"And the next day, the Ceremony of the Great Betting will start. Each will bring something that is the product of their toil, that which one is in the habit of using. And they will lay wagers one against another, and they will keep up the strength of the noise when the betting is in progress, and at that time they will be amusing my mind.

"So when you assemble you will give greetings and thanksgiving to all these things mentioned. Now another thing. It will be the duty of all people that they will possess the power to be happy, and they will be in the habit of giving thanks when they see that all my work continues to please the minds of the children, even to the least, and that you all have an equal right to it.

"All of you have an equal right to this which I have created. You will continue to comfort one another, and you will greet one another with thanksgiving when you will visit another's lodges and when you meet one another on the path

Johe'koh

that shall always be the principle thing, that happiness of life shall be the foremost matter. You will greet one another with thanksgiving. You will also greet me with thanksgiving.

"When this is done we will all habitually have peace of mind. Do not ever forget this in the future. If it should happen that you will forget the importance of peace of mind, you will not continue to live, and your children will not continue to live. Now you will attend to each other's thinking here on the earth, and the reason I have done this is that the time is coming closer when my brother and I will disagree.

"I believe he will try to let loose on the earth things which will kill human beings. That is why I have left things among the people upon which they should live. Now it will happen in the days to come that there will be divisions and disagreements among the families of human beings. There will be nothing but disputes, and they will forget happiness and peace, and they will also forget about me. At that time people will destroy one another, and the ties of blood among families will die out, and at that time you will see that the path in the sky (the Milky Way) will divide and there will be two minds among the people on the earth.

"Now I will depart for home. I will hear, however, when people will speak to me. It will come to pass that I will return in the future and it may happen that my brother's efforts to control everything may not succeed." Then he departed for home.

Youngtree and Inseparable Flower followed Skyholder's original instructions. They carried out the ceremonies at the appointed times and sought to bring their minds together as one mind in thanksgiving for all the things which supported their lives. For some time they were all of one mind in what they did and they were surprised one night when they saw that the visible path in the sky (the Milky Way) was divided. Not long after disagreements appeared among them. Now they

Johe'koh

took opposite sides in all kinds of matters and the minds separated until it was not possible for them to perform the Four Ceremonies.

Youngtree spoke among the people, urging them to remember the admonitions of the Skyholder, warning that if the people fail to remember to be grateful and to value peace, and also peaceful minds, that human beings would be unable to live. But his words were not successful and the people continued to be divided.

This continued for some time. Then mysterious things began to happen. Individuals would now frequently disappear. Human beings were known to kill one another. There was an eclipse of the sun and of the moon and among the families of human beings there was no peace. Some of the children disappeared, and no one knew where they went.

Now it happened that the people heard a loud noise from the west and the Thunder Voices were loud and then it rained and lightning appeared. For three days without stop it rained and the people became fearful. After a while the rain stopped, and there appeared at that time a rainbow which had one end on the earth and the other in the sky. There were colors which they, perhaps, had not seen before.

The people went to Youngtree's lodge and asked, "What does it mean?"

"I think it is a sign. We have not done that which Skyholder designed for us. I believe that he has returned, as he said he would."

Not long after that, Skyholder arrived there. The people did not recognize him.

"I have come here because there is strife among you. Now there are two minds (modes of thought) which have come to earth, and also two minds direct the lives of human beings. You have seen what has happened. You have disagreed, and now you saw the path in the sky has become

Johe'koh

divided. It is a sign that beginning now there shall continue to be discord among people. The path in the sky has divided to accommodate this discord.

"My power is symbolized by the rainbow which you have now seen. Everything -- the people, the things that are growing, and the animals, and those with appointed overseeing duties, must take note of it. In the very distant future it will happen that you will see a rainbow come forth from the place of the sunrise and passing through the middle of the sky to the place of the sunset. Then the earth will end and everything placed here for your protection will also end.

"Until then I have given the duty to the Thunder Voices, that they will bring forth the rains which will cleanse the earth. When this happens, everything will be renewed. My work here will receive new life. The symbol of this is that from time to time you will see the rainbow. It will continue to be so as long as my work continues on the earth.

"Now I remind you that there was a time when I was here on the earth and it was here that my power grew from its own sources. When I was here I used a bow and arrow, and here grows that from which that bow and arrow were made. And here also grows the yellow sunflower, the first source of light on the earth. And here the red willow, the first plant on the earth. The Great Bluebird was the first animate being. Therefore there were the first three colors in the world. This is why I have chosen to make the rainbow a symbol, so that when the rains come and the rainbow appears, you shall continue to remember me forever.

"Now I will add to the Four Ceremonies which I gave you. When the season changes and spring begins, you will again see wild strawberries, the small kind. You should gather berries and the entire community shall assemble yourselves. When all are assembled, a drink will be made of the berries and you will choose two persons, a male and a female. They

Johe'koh

will go around the assembly and distribute the berry juice among the people. These two will be young people just coming to maturity.

"At that time each will take up the drink and will give thanksgiving to me and you will drink the juice of the fruit. Then, when this is done, the Feather Dance will take place. It will be your custom that everyone will make a circuit and all shall be happy, thinking, 'I am grateful to be alive and in peace.'

"And the same will happen when the raspberry ripens. When you see it has ripened, you will collect it and the whole community will assemble and you will prepare the juice. The ceremony will be exactly the same as with the strawberries.

"There will be fruits which will ripen after this. The mulberry shall be joined with the Green Corn Festival. When the ceremonies take place, the first thing that will make a circuit of the people will be the mulberry juice, and all will drink of it. When the ceremony starts, the juice should be placed at the center of the assembly, and each individual will take and drink of it and will give thanksgiving as they do so.

"Now I have assigned the women to assist one another. I have assigned to a certain tree that it shall give forth a sap which will be called sugar. When the days are beginning to become warm, the maple tree will give off sap and it will be good that the people will drink the sap and you will do the same things that you did when you assembled the ceremony for the fruit.

"I will visit the earth at some time in the future. Now I have placed among you a very important matter. Love. You will continue to love one another. Then there will be peace." Then Skyholder disappeared, and no one knew where he went.

For a time the ceremonies were carried on correctly, but it happened that once again there began to be

Johe'koh

disagreements among the people even about how to perform the ceremonies. Some people said, "I am doing this the correct way and I will do as I please." This went on for a long time.

Then it happened that when people traveled about in the forest, they began to see animals they did not know. Some of these animals were ugly. These monsters began to kill people. When they went far from home, people were killed by the monsters. More and more were all kinds of things befalling the people. Only a few were conducting the ceremonies.

Now these unfortunate occurrences were becoming more frequent and people were living in a continuous state of grief. In time, the ceremonies were performed no more. At this time they were surprised that Skyholder appeared once again.

"I have come for only a short time and this is the last time I will come to earth. From now on, the people will know only my name. Now I have come to explain what has happened. My brother has begun to let loose his work here upon the earth and also in the minds of human beings. He will try to spoil all kinds of things which I have created. It would be a good thing if you would continue to highly prize the Four Ceremonies, and also that you continue to love one another. Do not forget love, and also peace. You must also always remember me day after day and night after night." And at that time he departed.

Johe'koh

SEVEN
THE CLANS

Many people knew the history of what had happened and what had been foretold for the future. Many also used the sweat lodges to forecast the future. Now sickness came and adults and children died. People became insane, and others reviled one another by gossip. There were instances wherein people antagonized one another and even committed murder.

It came to pass that there were none who respected one another among the families. The Four Ceremonies were no longer performed. The only things which flourished were those which vexed peoples minds. It had reached the point where the women and children did nothing but weep and there was nothing in the minds of the people but fear. At that point they noticed that the amount of fruit that grew had decreased. Season after season, the fruits diminished.

At that time it was reported that Skyholder had been seen among the people. Not long afterwards it became known that this report was indeed true. At that period, one would think, the discord among humans would have diminished somewhat in force, that all minds had quieted down.

Skyholder reappeared. "Now all must assemble. Now you have seen what has happened. You people do not love one another at all. You do not seem to be aware of the thing which has caused all this misery. My brother has caused all of this. He pursues his work in accordance with his objectives, and he desires to spoil everything I have created.

"You must understand what I am saying. You must stop your habit of disrespecting one another. You must take up love and peace here on the earth. You will be able to do so. You will be able to love one another.

"Now it has come to pass that there are two paths. One is for the human beings who have completed the ceremonies, who are good people, who have cultivated love and peace. When they have exhausted their days on the earth, they will depart for the sky world where they will find happiness. They will arrive at that place where the Four Ceremonies are being continuously performed.

"Now I believe the other path is that which will be followed by those who have not forsaken that which is wrong -- the handiwork of my brother who has a hateful mind. When such people reach the end of their allotted days, they will follow this path to my brother's lodge and in that place one will see forever that which is ruinous.

"You who live on the earth have a great duty to perform, and you will need to try hard to succeed. If you fail in mind, you will perish on the earth, and also in the place of ruin, so that one who fails in this matter will die twice. We can do nothing to stop the misfortune which has happened. I have come to give you that which you can use so that you can continue to live. It is called medicine. The reason I am doing this is that now disease will travel over the earth. Diseases will destroy many people. My brother has caused it to be. Now I deliver at your side medicines which may in some small way prove to be a preventive.

"Now bring to me one of each of the various kinds of grasses and shrubs, and of the trees." Now the people collected these things and brought them to Skyholder.

Clans

"Now," Skyholder said, "You know the various names of these plants." Then he held a plant aloft and said, "This will be for medicine, and will be able to counteract a few of the kinds of disease." And he saw that there were only a few people who could remember the names of the plants correctly. "In the future, there will be only a few people who will know the medicines that can aid people. They will continue to aid the people, both in flesh and in mind. Now you see next to you the native tobacco, and this will work together with the medicine plants. When one becomes sick, one will take the tobacco to a person who one chooses as knowledgeable in the medicines. Then one will ask for help, and will give the tobacco to the other.

"The person who knows medicine will take the tobacco and will go to the place where the medicine grows and then will explain their purpose to the plants and the name of the person who needs help. Then they will cast the tobacco onto the fire in thanksgiving and then, and not before then, one will take up the medicine. Then you will address me in the sky world for aid so that they may recover.

"There is another matter. When the earth grows warm you must apply hard labor to this task. You will learn the custom of planting. You will have the corn, beans and squash. When you plant, you will make use of the ceremony of which you have become accustomed, repeatedly giving thanksgiving. The Great Feather Dance will take place. When the plants have sprouted you will continue by taking care of them and when they are ready you will again employ a ceremony to give a thanksgiving. Thus, when the green beans are ready, you will put aside a kettle of these cooked, enough for the entire assembly, and then one will be appointed to speak with a unanimous voice in the ceremony of thanksgiving. And the same shall happen when the green corn

Clans

is ready and the squash puts forth fruit.

"Those who have followed my instructions and who have continued to esteem greatly the ceremonies and to have love for others and for peace will one day depart the earth and take that path to the place where I reside. In that place there is no sickness, and one is not required to struggle for the things which sustain one's life, and no one there is sorrowful, and only that which can give pleasure to the mind is found there. All the kinds of fruits and flowers, all the trees and shrubs, all the animals and all the dwellers of the sky whom you have never seen on the earth, all are there. When one shall arrive there after departing from earth, one shall become possessed of all these joys, and that condition shall continue to give pleasure to one's mind forever.

"I have said there are two paths. There is one path which is reserved for those who do not love other people, and do not love peace. Those people will arrive at my brother's lodge, and they will see great suffering, and they will be famished, and will suffer my brother's fate forever. I have used his anger to kindle a fire far hotter than the fires on earth because he wants to control the minds of human beings on the earth. Now I have told you about both things. Whichever path one chooses, one must obey its destiny.

"Now I am leaving the earth for the last time. It may come to pass that you will again forget to love one another, and peace. The next time, I will send another person to aid you. Only twice shall it be repeated that I will send a messenger to you. When the third comes, you will see what shall happen on the earth. Long before the end, you will see that the things upon which you live will gradually decrease in quantity, all the things on earth that grow will become weaker, and finally it will happen that nothing more can grow.

"The same will happen to the animals and the birds.

Clans

They will also grow fewer in number until at some future time you will see no more of them. And at that time awe-inspiring things will happen. There will be earthquakes and things which have great power which now abide in the earth will come forth and they will be more powerful than human beings. I believe my brother has the power to seduce the minds of human beings and then all will become spoiled and destitute on the earth.

"Now I will prepare to return to my home. I will fix my path on the earth, and at the end of that path you will find corn and beans and squashes. Do not waste them. All shall share these things. These are the Three Sisters, and you will continue to live upon them. You shall address them, saying "Our Mothers," for they will all care for you to the end.

"You will choose two young people, male and female, who have grown to the point where he is just beginning to change his voice and she has begun to deny herself certain things. They will go to the place where I have gone. When they have arrived where my path will have ended, they will find beside an open grave a mound of earth upon which will be growing a corn plant, a bean plant, and a squash plant, symbols of your lives.

"The woman shall be first. She will take the corn, and next the bean, and the man will take the squash. And when they have done this, they will understand the meaning of the grave. This is what lies at the end of the path of every human being when you shall depart from the earth. But afterwards, you human beings who remain will keep things in good order. There is one thing I hide from you. Normally no one will know the number of his or her days. And I hide from you the path and the place to which I have gone.

"I will henceforth have my eyes fixed on your ways of thinking. I will hear if one will think of me and that one shall

Clans

greet me with thanksgiving, and that one might ask something of me. I leave now. You will keep your eyes fixed on the place I go.

Then he left and the people kept their eyes fixed on him until they lost sight of him. The elders listened and they chose two people to follow Skyholder's path on the earth as they had been told. Now these two saw plainly the tracks he had left and they followed the trail westward. Soon the trail ended and the two saw the plants and the woman took up the corn and bean plants, and the man took up the squash plant, and the man said, "Here there seems to be a heap of earth. One must presume that He lies under here, his head to the west, his feet to the east."

When they returned to the assembly of people, they were asked to tell their story. They related their experience in finding the corn, bean, and squash plants and they delivered these to the people.

At that time the Elders said, "You have gone to a great deal of trouble to get these things. We assembled here have made preparations to greet you with thanksgiving now that you have completed the task of bringing Our Mothers here. We now with one voice give thanksgiving. We shall now go along the path of ritual he has set out for us. Also, we will greet with thanksgiving all the things which support our lives. What shall we do with these things which have come among us?"

Then someone said, "I think we all have an equal right to them. It would be a good thing if we all assist one another when we plant, and again when we must cultivate and then at harvest. When we have plenty, we will divide it up among us." After that the people helped one another in this work.

Spring came early at that time. Then the elders said, "We will seek aid through the Great Gamble. Our Mothers,

Clans

the Three Sisters, the corn, beans and squash, shall be the chief personalities represented at this time. We will wager for them, and after the game, we will plant. Then we shall do as Skyholder has ordered done."

Another came forward with an idea. "This will be a good thing. We will commemorate that which happened in the past, when Skyholder and his Grandmother, Mature Blossoms, bet together. The two wagered all that which grows on the earth. So the way we will do this, we menfolk will wager against our mothers, the women."

The elders agreed to the matter. Now they did play the game, and the male human beings won and now they said, "It shall come to pass, when these anniversaries recur, the first thing to be done is that the Great Gamble will be performed. At that time, our Mothers shall become the central persons."

Now the people planted and when they finished they assembled and held a great Feather dance. They offered up thanksgiving for having finished planting their fields.

When the seeds sprouted, the people hoed their gardens and then gathered together. They gave thanks that the seeds had sprouted, and they held the Great Feather Dance. It was decided that there would be performed another ceremony when the harvest was in and for a long time the people were at peace.

Then it happened that tragedy struck among the people. People began to die. Those who passed away were buried, but then another, who was not sick at all, passed on. There was tremendous sadness at these frequent and numerous deaths. Because of this sadness, there were many who did not attend the Four Ceremonies celebrations, and these were becoming less and less fully performed.

The elders grew concerned and they called an assembly. They explained that the deaths had caused such a

Clans

sadness that the world was in crisis, and they asked the people assembled to propose a plan that might lift the sadness. Finally a young man, one with the body of a youth, stood up and said, "I have decided that I should try to suggest a proposition as to what we should do. Now we have seen that there are many different things in the world -- the shrubs, the grasses, the trees. All have exclusive duties to perform, all are alive. There are different kinds of birds and animals. They differ among themselves, and we should emulate them. Now it is time that we should form clans. We have become numerous, and we should apportion the body of people. There should be a limited number of clans, and they should call themselves cousins in the future.

"The clans should become the chief means we will employ in the matters befalling us now because we are separating ourselves from one another. When a death occurs among a Sisterhood -- a clan -- the minds of the opposite sisterhood will be clear and they (the second sisterhood) will arise as one and go to the place where one has been lost. It shall be the duty of the unaffected sisterhood to utter words which will repeatedly cheer up and encourage those who have suffered loss and to comfort those who have become enshrouded in darkness.

"I have proposed that it is evident that among the grasses and the shrubs there are those who are different from one another. There are clans of grasses and of trees and of animals. So now the matter is with you."

The elders considered the matter for some time. Finally they decided to adopt the proposal that the entire body of the people would be divided into diverse clans. So the custom is to be thus: no matter which sisterhood suffers loss, the other sisterhood will then be responsible for everything. The other will attend to everything. It will be their duty to

Clans

speak, and they will encourage the minds of those who remain alive, so that their minds will become settled again.

The elders discussed how to put the proposal into existence for a long time, but they were not successful in devising a plan whereby such diverse clans could be created. Finally they decided to ask the young man who had first made the proposal for suggestions about how it could be carried out. They addressed the young man, saying "We have not been successful. You have obviously given much thought to this proposal. We are therefore putting responsibility for it in your hands. You are hereby given power to enact a plan."

The young man replied, "Tomorrow, assemble all the people. When the sun is at midday, all the people must be assembled. I shall arrange matters so there are diverse clans. The women of the nations will be the principle ones in this matter. The oldest woman of each of these families will lead her entire family here. When they arrive, we will go to the stream. By tomorrow, that which we are seeking to do will be accomplished."

The people were ready and assembled the following day. At midday the young man said, "Now we are all here present. I have been invested with the authority to direct this matter. Now I shall lead, and we will all go to the river."

The people followed, grouped in their (female side) families. Toward evening they arrived at the river. At the river's edge there stood a tall tree from which a grape vine was attached. He placed his hands on it and pulled and threw it to the opposite side of the river, where it was then affixed. Now the vine was stretched across the river and it was used to help people cross over. Then he said, "The eldest women of your families will come here in the morning and will fetch water for cooking. When she dips for water, she must be careful to notice what kind of thing she will see, and she must

Clans

not forget it. I will come here in the morning. Now you must follow me when we cross the river."

At that time they started. They went to the spot where the grape vine crossed the water, and one by one they crossed as fast as possible. Suddenly, when the sun set, the vine broke and floated away. Now there were people on both sides of the stream. Now they made camps on each side of the water.

Early the next morning, all hastened to get water at the flowing stream. The young man came and the elders followed. They went to the camp of the eldest woman and asked, "What kind of thing have you seen since you arose?" She answered, "I went to dip water at the river and as I dipped I saw a deer standing near by. I then returned home."

And he said, "The animal you have seen was created by the one who finished our bodies, the Creator, and moreover that is now the name of your clan. Just as water flows in a certain direction, just as the sun follows a certain path, so it will come to pass that your family will come to esteem the name so much that they will say, 'We are of the deer clan.'"

He approached another headwoman and he asked her the same question, and she replied she had seen a bear. Her's became the bear clan. They were to become brother and sister to the deer clan. He approached another, and she said she had seen a snipe. They became the snipe clan, brothers and sisters to the deer and bear clans. Another woman had seen an eel. She was now the headwoman of the eel clan, brother and sister to the deer, bear, and snipe clans.

Now they departed, the young man and the ancient ones, and this time they arrived at the river. Again he pulled up a grapevine, and again cast it across the river. He crossed and they followed him. At the first camp, he said to the headwoman, "What kind of wonderful thing have you seen?"

Clans

"I saw a wolf running there" she replied, and her family became the wolf clan. They approached another and she had seen a beaver. They became the beaver clan. The next had seen a turtle, and they became the turtle clan.

Now he came to another woman and he asked what she had seen. "When I went to get water," she said, "I saw a bear cub walking in the mud."

"Now it has gone amiss," he said. "We already have a bear clan on the other side of the river. Now there are two bear clans. Sometime in the future, it may need to be reconsidered. The two bear clans should make but one group. You are of the Small Bear clan, and will be known as such from now on. Also, you and the families I have passed on this side of the river are brothers and sisters. You join the Turtle, Wolf, and Beaver clans on this side of the river, and will sit with them on one side of the fire. Those on the other side you will address as 'Cousins.'"

The people were then assembled, and they took their seats according to the clan designations, with each of the two cousins on opposite sides of the fire. Then the young man announced, "There is an unfinished business. You must first consider what to do because there are two bear clans. And you must decide which of the two clans must cross over the fire."

The elders gathered in council and considered this question for some time. Finally they announced, "Since the ancient bears customarily roam about, and the cub bears customarily remain at home, it should be the ancient bear clan that crosses the fire." And it happened that the Bear clan crossed the fire to join the Bear Cub clan.

Now the elders said, "We have completed the matter. But there is another. What about the family across the river that you did not visit?"

The young man called the eldest woman of the family

Clans

to his side and asked her what she had seen that morning. She replied that she had seen a hawk. "Now," he announced, "you are of the Hawk clan."

"Now there are things you must remember. You who are of the Deer Clan, do not forget that the clanship shall follow the female lineage, and that the women are the rulers. It is in the persons of the women that the human beings who are going to pause on the earth are being formed. You must give names to all your members, and your clan will have names which are specific to the clan."

These rules were stated for each of the clans. "That which we have arranged," the young man said, "is so durable that it will last as long as our families will continue to exist. It will last as long as the grasses grow and the trees grow. It will last as long as the rivers flow. Now I have finished arranging your affairs."

The eldest man of the Wolf clan now stood and said, "The young man standing here has completed the rules which will govern the assembly here. Should anyone address him they will call him Ho'nigo(n)heowa'ne(n), His-Mind-Is-Great. We must try to always remember him." And the elders honored him and made speeches in thanksgiving and sang the Personal Chant in his honor. The entire assembly of people stood and held their arms upward, and shouted three times. He said, "Now the whole matter is finished."

Now the people dispersed, and they re-crossed the river. At that time Ho'nigo(n)heowa'ne, His-Mind-Is-Great, said, "It shall continue to be in the future, that there will always be clans on both sides of the river."

Clans

Appearances

98

Bibliography

Thomas S. Abler, ed., "The Indians of Old Dradition," MIN, no. 24, 1982, 71-87.

Joseph Le Caron, In Christien Le Clercq, *First Establishment of the Faith in New France,* trans. John Gilmary Shea, New York, 1881, 216-217.

Harriet Maxwell Converse, *Myths and Legends of the New York State Iroquois,* ed. Arthur Caswell Parker, NYSMB, no. 125, Albany, 1908, 32-36.

L. Hennepin, *A New Discovery of a Vast Country in America,* London, 1698, II, 48-50.

J.N.B. Hewitt, "Iroquois Cosmology," pt. 1, Bureau of American Ethnology, *Annual Report, 1899-1900,* Washington, D.C., 1903, 141-220, with an Onondaga version by John Buck of the Grand River recorded in 1889, a Seneca version by John Armstrong of the Cattaraugus Territory in 1896, a Mohawk version by Seth Newhouse in 1896.

Carl F. Klinck and James J. Talman, eds., *The Journal of Major John Norton,* 1816, Toronto: The Champlain Society, 1970 at 88-98.

Joseph Francois Lafiteau, *Customs of the American Indians Compared With the Customs of Primitive Times,* edited and translated by William N. Fenton and Elizabeth I. Moore, Toronto, 1974-1977, I, 81-83.

Johannes Megapolensis, Jr., "A Short Account of the Mohawk Indians" (1644) in NNN, 177-178. http://historical.library.cornell.edu/cgi-bin/cul.nys/docviewer?did=nys175&seq=2&frames=0&view=text

Gabriel Sagard, *The Long Journey to the Country of the Hurons,* ed. George M. Wrong, trans. H.H. Langton ,Toronto, 1939, (orig. pub. Paris 1632,) 169-170.http://www.champlainsociety ca/cs_bibliography .htm

Henry R. Schoolcraft, *Notes on the Iroquois; or Contributions to the Statistics, Aboriginal History, Antiquities, and General Ethnology of Western New-York* (New York, 1846) 36-37.

.